THE CELTS
CONQUERORS OF ANCIENT EUROPE

Christiane Eluère

DISCOVERIES
HARRY N. ABRAMS, INC., PUBLISHERS

SEPVLTVRE
DE LA MOTTE S^T VALENTIN
COVRCELLES EN MONTAGNE. HTE MARNE
DECOVVERTE PAR Henri MILLON
XIX IVIN MDCCCLXXX.

CONTENTS

Between 900 and 600 BC, at the close of the Bronze Age, ancestors of the Celts founded a new culture. Across most of the European continent, warriors carrying swords and riding on horseback displayed a new kind of power. The Celts mastered iron, and from this new material were forged weapons of such great value that their owners carried them to their graves.

CHAPTER I

BIRTH OF A WARRIOR ARISTOCRACY

Celtic princes' graves abounded in such tokens of refinement and wealth as this wine jar and drinking vessel (painting opposite), found in the barrow, or burial mound, of La Motte-St.-Valentin, in northeastern France, or this odd little bronze figure (right), with its breastplate and arm rings, from Hallstatt, in Austria.

In 1771 a cauldron containing over 65 pounds of gold coins and a golden torque, or neck piece, came to light at Podmokly, in Bohemia (now part of the Czech Republic), and attracted the attention of scholars everywhere. While all of Europe had enthused about the legend of Ossian, a 3rd-century AD Gaelic (meaning an Irish or Scottish Celt) bard rediscovered by the Scottish poet James Macpherson (1736–96), it was through the study of this and other finds that interest in the Celts began in earnest.

The cauldron from Podmokly (above), shown with a few coins from the hoard, in an engraving made in the year of its discovery (1771). It is encircled by a torque, a twisted metal collar worn by Celtic warriors and deities.

As the field of archaeology developed during the 19th century, it became the chief source of knowledge about the Celts and revealed a past shared among the different regions of Europe, including the British Isles. The ancient texts—though numerous and explicit—took second place to the sheer abundance of archaeological evidence.

Among the first discoveries of Celtic archaeology was this sandstone pillar (left) from Pfalzfeld, Germany, found in 1608. It was originally topped by a head and would then have stood about 8 feet high. Unprotected until 1934, it now measures only about 5 feet. It dates from 450 to 350 BC and probably stood on a barrow.

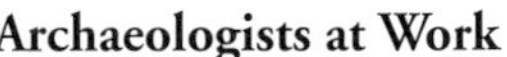

Archaeologists at Work

In 1824 came the first signs of the existence of an important Iron Age cemetery at Hallstatt, a village in central Austria; ancient salt mines had been found there as early as the 14th century. Then, in 1857, excavations near the Lake of Neuchâtel, in western Switzerland, led to the discovery of stores of arms and personal

Hallstatt (left) is a small, completely isolated site in the heart of the Salzkammergut region of Upper Austria and is accessible only by river. The climate there is harsh, with little sunlight. Yet the site was very busy between the 7th and 5th centuries BC, probably because of its salt mines. The area possessed all the right conditions for a new civilization to emerge and for its remains to be preserved. Two thousand graves have been excavated in Hallstatt's astonishing early Celtic cemetery.

ornaments at La Tène, the shallows at the east end of the lake. Hallstatt and La Tène became sites whose names were used to denote the Early (800–500 BC) and Late (500 BC–AD 200) Iron Ages, respectively.

At the end of the century many similar grave mounds were explored in Austria, southern Germany, Switzerland, and eastern France. Meanwhile, in 1874 German archaeologist Heinrich Schliemann (1822–90) discovered the treasures of the ancient city of Mycenae, in Greece. And southeast of Rome, at Praeneste, a rich Etruscan tomb was also unearthed. The concept of "princely" protohistoric tombs and that of parallel development among Iron Age societies, whether in Italy or in central Europe, took hold.

La Tène, located by the side of the Lake of Neuchâtel, in Switzerland, was once an important meeting place. In 1857 antiques enthusiast Hansli Kopp found some very odd iron weapons there. The exceptional quantity of weapons recovered since then has justified archaeologists in regarding it as a representative site for the period of the greatest Celtic expansion. Battlefield, market, or sanctuary? Successive excavation campaigns have failed to determine the exact function of this Late Iron Age center.

An Early Iron Age barrow topped by a sandstone statue at Kilchberg, in western Germany.

Contemporary Investigation

Excavation of Celtic burial sites in Europe persisted during the 20th century and continued to produce sensational finds. The opening of the tomb at Vix, a site in eastern central France, in 1953, and the discovery there of an enormous bronze krater (a jar or vase for mixing wine and water), was a major event in world archaeology. In 1978 a barrow at Hochdorf, near Stuttgart, Germany—minutely excavated and then studied in the laboratory—yielded valuable information about its occupant's standard of living.

A new wave of excavations soon shed some light on Celtic settlements: the Heuneburg, a fortified site on the west bank of the Danube in southwestern Germany; the fortified town of Manching, in southeastern Germany; and Mont Beuvray, in central France. Sanctuaries also began to be studied, such as those found in Entremont and Roquepertuse, in southern France; Gournay-sur-Aronde, in northern France; Fellbach-Schmiden, in western Germany; and Snettisham, in central England.

Laboratory science made its own contributions through dendrochronology (a method of dating wood by studying trees' growth rings) and the analysis of the remains of textiles, metals, and organic substances.

Protohistory and the "Urnfields"

The Bronze and Iron ages make up what is known as protohistory. These names, convenient because they refer to the technical evolution of the societies in question, were bestowed during the 19th century. At that time a sharp break between the two ages was believed to have occurred. Nowadays it is thought that the transition—in about the 8th century BC in western Europe—took place gradually, with a wide range of minor variations among different communities.

Similarly, the famous "Urnfield" theory (named after a type of cremation cemetery), which held that the proto-Celts were invaders from the east between the 13th and 8th centuries BC, has now been abandoned. It is now agreed that the Celts evolved from populations already residing in Europe during the Bronze Age. In the 13th and 12th centuries BC we find that a few Bronze Age graves already prefigure the spectacular burial sites of the first Celtic princes. In the 11th century BC appeared bronze equipment that was clearly intended for devotional offerings: breastplates from the French sites of Fillinges (in the southeast) and Marmesse (in the northeast), as well as wheels, shields, and helmets in many other areas of Europe.

Two or three centuries earlier, symbols of prestige had appeared, heralding the splendor of the 6th century BC: the four-wheeled cart depicted on a funerary urn from Sublaines, in western France (opposite), for example, or breastplates found at Marmesse (left). This large pectoral with a bird and wheels (above), from a forest in the Jura mountain range between France and Switzerland, combines traditional Bronze Age motifs with Celtic exuberance.

The End of the Bronze Age

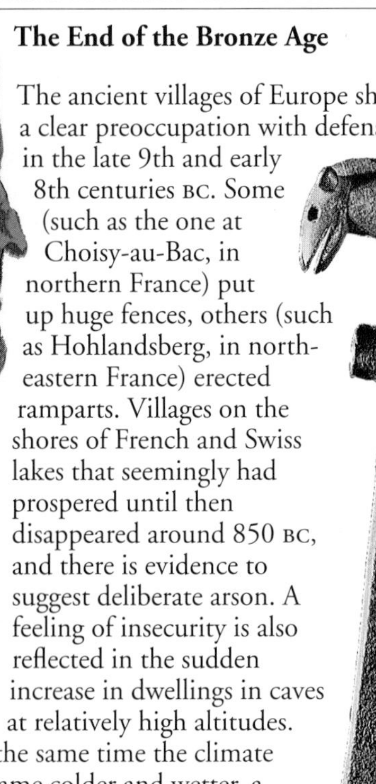

The ancient villages of Europe show a clear preoccupation with defense in the late 9th and early 8th centuries BC. Some (such as the one at Choisy-au-Bac, in northern France) put up huge fences, others (such as Hohlandsberg, in northeastern France) erected ramparts. Villages on the shores of French and Swiss lakes that seemingly had prospered until then disappeared around 850 BC, and there is evidence to suggest deliberate arson. A feeling of insecurity is also reflected in the sudden increase in dwellings in caves at relatively high altitudes. At the same time the climate became colder and wetter, a trend that was to continue until the 6th century BC. Trade networks thinned out for unknown reasons, and manufacturing activity was affected. The production of gold objects began to slacken. Bronze goods were carefully salvaged and buried in hoards. Whether economic or social, there was certainly a crisis.

A small bronze figurine adorns a ritual ax from Hallstatt (two views at left). Horsemen and cattle were favored decorative themes during the 7th century BC in this dynamic area of central Europe, which served as a melting pot for influences from all sides of the Alps.

The New Caste of Horsemen

It was at this point—in the 9th and 8th centuries BC—that the first signs of a previously unknown order appeared: horsemen armed with long swords.

These horsemen are found sporadically at burial sites, accompanied by exotic imported items, burial wagons, and gold—all of which foreshadow a new ruling class. Riding on horseback, for instance, was one of the innovations that denoted power. In the cemetery at Chavéria, in the Jura mountains, some twenty barrows have been excavated. Five contained long "Hallstattian" swords, pieces of harnesses, and, in one grave, there was a bronze bowl with a beaded rim that is curiously similar to ones produced in the 8th century BC in northern Italy.

In 1987 the discovery of a remarkable grave under a barrow at the site of St.-Romain-de-Jalionas, in southeastern France, provided crucial information about conditions in the 9th and 8th centuries BC: Traditional objects still in use were being adapted to new rites, already very similar to those of the 6th century. The warrior was buried, not yet with a wagon, but with his long bronze sword, gold ornaments, and a drinking set (usually a wine jar, a vase for mixing wine and water, and a cup) also in bronze: all objects

Found in a warrior's grave of 400 BC at Hallstatt, this decorated sword scabbard (detail above) illustrates the high status of horsemen. A central frieze shows three foot soldiers with shields followed by four mounted warriors carrying lances and wearing breastplates or jerkins and a skirt over trousers of some sort. Their shoes have upturned toes, and they wear protective helmets. At each side two wrestlers hold a wheel, a traditional symbol of prosperity. The tip of the scabbard depicts an erotic scene involving humans and animals.

that had previously tended to be reserved for devotional offerings, or which had been found arranged in groups—whether for purposes of ritual or concealment—in Late Bronze Age hoards.

A cylindrical bucket nearly 14 inches tall from Magny-Lambert (left). This type of bronze vessel was found both north of the Alps and in Italy from the 8th century BC onward.

Long Swords

Weapons with iron blades, superseding earlier bronze models, were—along with riding on horseback—the distinctive marks of eminent warriors in the 7th century BC. Many such weapons found at Hallstatt confirm they were signs of privilege, with hilts covered in gold leaf or carved in ivory and inlaid with amber.

Weapons from graves at Hallstatt (opposite). The 7th-century BC swords with long iron blades imitate those of bronze. Their hilts were often embellished with ivory, amber, or gold.

Toward the end of the 8th and beginning of the 7th centuries BC, bronze vessels were often placed in graves alongside swords, as seen in burial sites at Magny-Lambert and Poiseul, in central France. By the end of the 7th century, wagons began to be placed in tombs.

The Jura region of present-day France, on the Swiss border, appears to mark the southwestern limit of the world of the Early Iron Age, although a few outlying settlements have been identified further west. To the east, especially in the salt-mining area around Hallstatt, were other cultural centers that had embarked upon a period of decisive expansion.

Fibulae (clasps) with double spirals (above) pinned the clothes of rich women at Hallstatt.

Lords of White Gold

In the Hallstatt cemetery, most of the two thousand excavated graves can be dated to the 7th and 6th

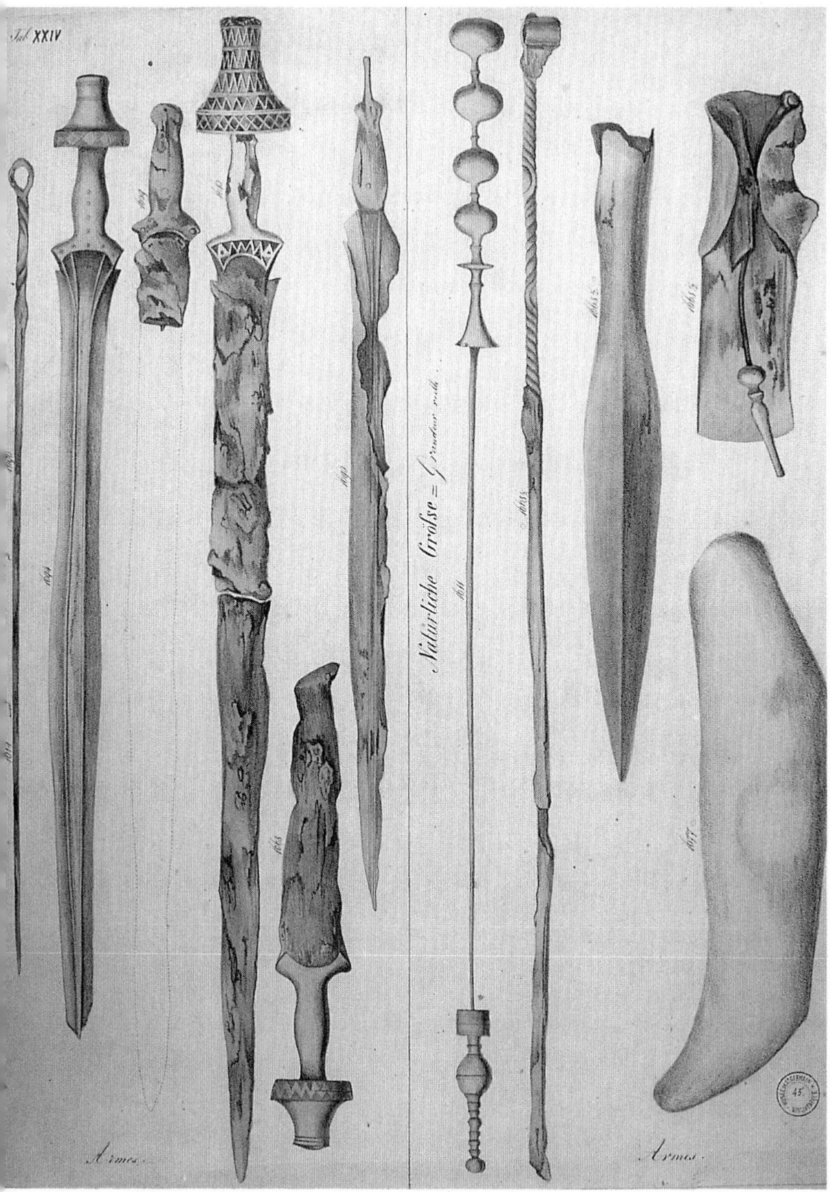
Tab. XXIV
Natürliche Grösse
Armes.
Armes.

centuries BC. Burials were slightly more common than cremations, but the latter provided the richer source of goods.

Warriors' graves made up only about a quarter of the Hallstatt cemetery, and of these only nineteen, from the 8th and 7th centuries BC, produced long swords and ceremonial axes. The more numerous 6th-century graves contained antenna daggers (so-called because of the shape of their openwork hilts). Women's graves tended to have masses of clanking jewelry and bulky fibulae in styles typical of the exuberant tastes of the period. Rich graves in the cemetery often contained impressive sets of bronze vessels—buckets, situlae (buckets with rims turned inward), bowls, and cups.

Hallstatt appears to have been a well-organized melting pot whose population came from many different areas. There were the salt miners themselves and the people in charge of them; woodcutters and carpenters—who collaborated in building the mine; merchants; tradespeople; and those responsible for the defense of the community. Together these people constructed a new model of a society in active contact with several different cultures.

Various pieces of clothing once worn by miners at Hallein have been found in an exceptional state of preservation because of the surrounding salt. This applies to the shoe shown below and to leather bonnets, also made of carefully stitched calfskin.

Salt as Preservative

The northern crest of the Alps contains rich reserves of salt. In place-names the element *hall,* a word of Celtic origin related to the German *salz* (salt), indicates ancient sites of salt exploitation in this area—Hall, Hallstatt, Hallein, and Reichenhall, for example. Salt was a form of wealth and object of long-distance trade. It preserves food and can be fed to livestock to strengthen them. Salt also effectively preserves organic remains. Items of clothing and protohistoric miners' equipment have survived intact, notably leather knapsacks used to transport blocks of the mineral.

As early as AD 1311 ancient relics from this site were already being accurately identified.

At first the Hallstattians extracted salt from the brine of natural springs through evaporation, but between the 8th and 6th centuries BC they developed the first and largest center for mining rock salt from the ground. Around 600 BC another big salt mine opened not far from Hallstatt, at Hallein (near Salzburg), a site that was more easily accessible. Hallstatt then went into decline: From the 5th century on it had fewer and less well furnished graves. The scene was now set for developments that were to take place in an area between eastern France and Austria, the focus of which was to reach markets south of the Alps.

Smitten by the finds at the Hallstatt cemetery, the grand duchess of Mecklenburg received permission from the Austrian emperor, Franz Josef I, to excavate there. She appears below tackling a grave in 1907.

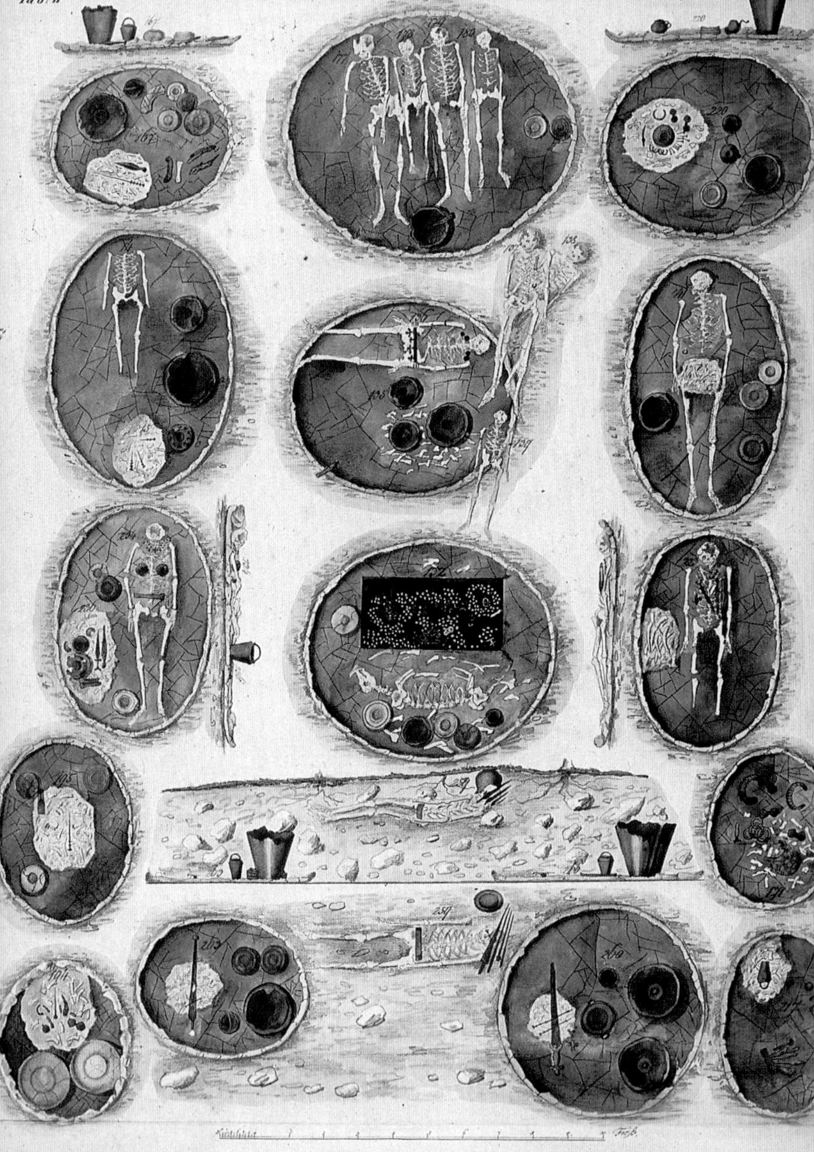
Tab: II

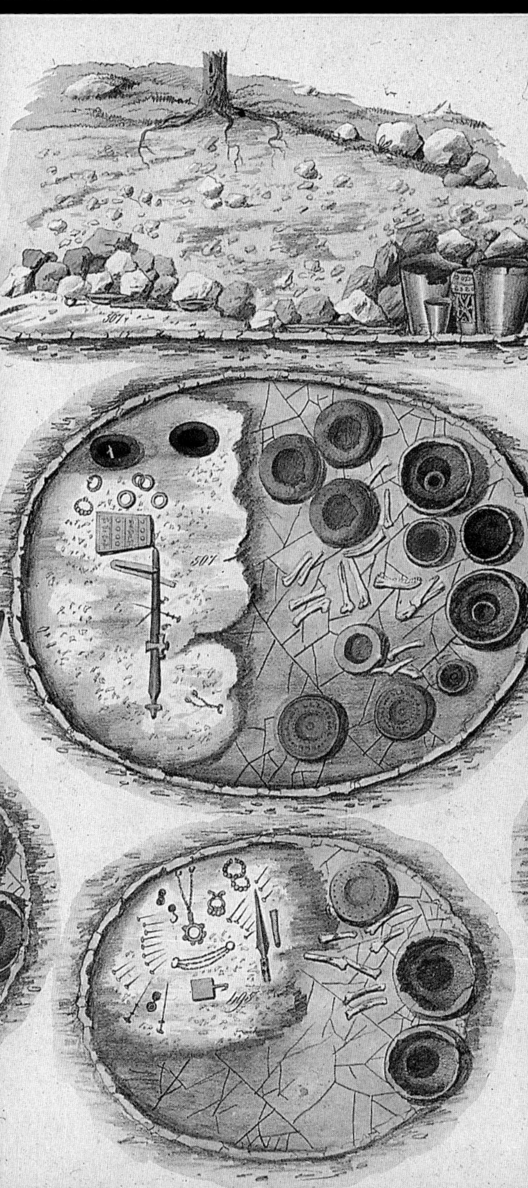

An Inveterate Excavator

Johann Georg Ramsauer, a mine surveyor, had a veritable field day when he began excavating the Hallstatt cemetery in 1846. Over the next seventeen years he explored 980 graves and unearthed 19,497 objects. He recorded all his observations in letters or notebooks, which were illustrated with watercolors by his friend Isidor Engel. Emperor Franz Josef and Empress Elizabeth attended the opening of grave 507, shown here, in person in October 1856. Ramsauer, who had had no formal training as an archaeologist, was advised by both the museum at Linz and experts in Vienna. Because he was the father of twenty-four children, he often suffered financial difficulties. Although he retained most of the excavated material, he, his wife, or his companions must sometimes have sold things to visitors passing through. This would explain why objects from Hallstatt can now be found all over the world.

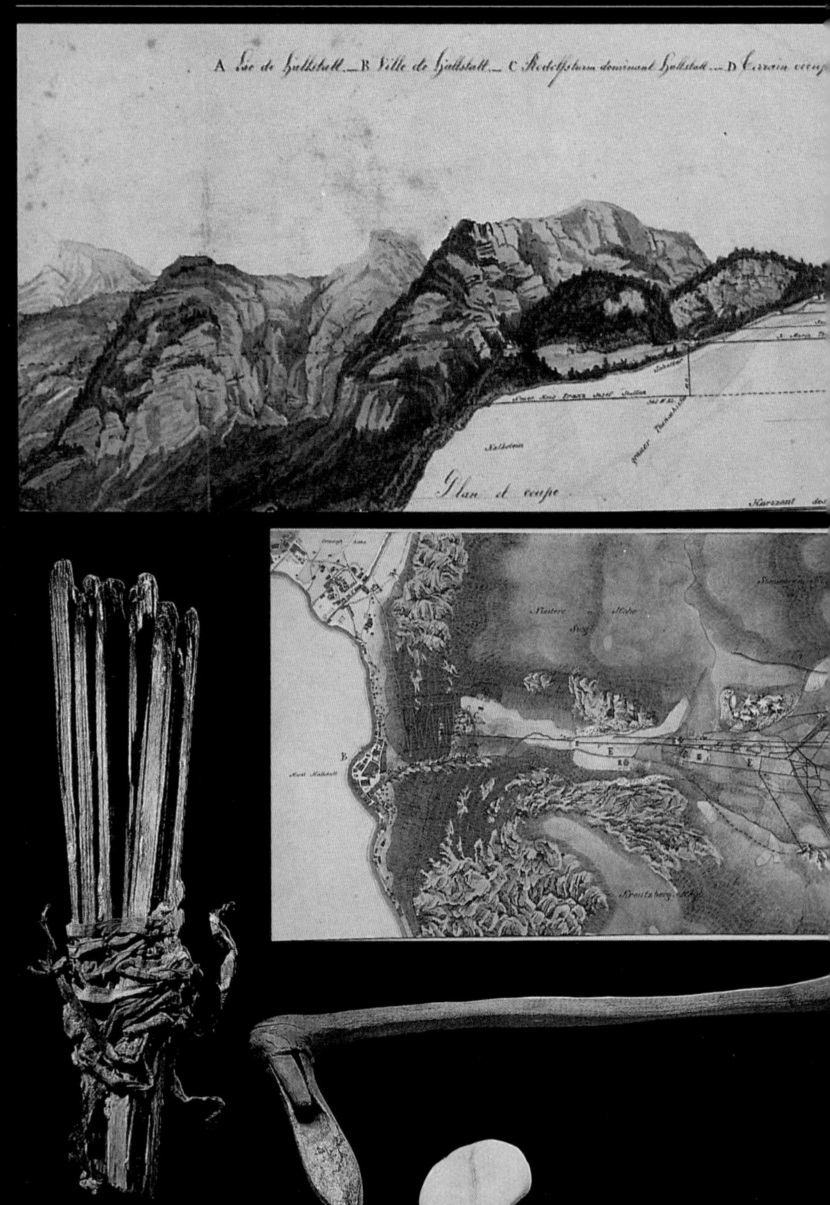
A Lac de Hallstatt _ B Ville de Hallstatt _ C Rodolfsturm dominant Hallstatt _ D Terrain
Plan et coupe

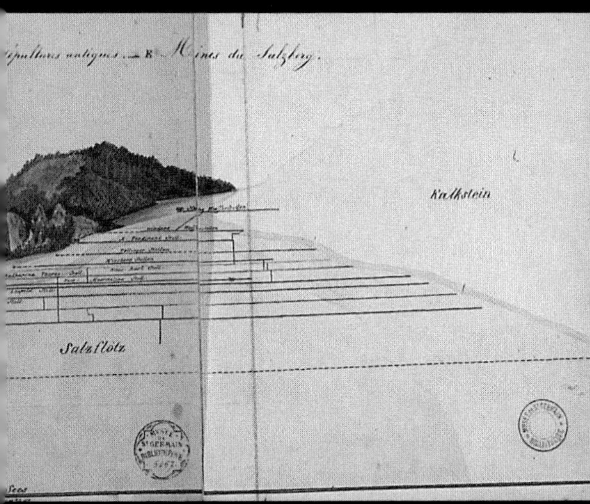

The Salt Mine

The underground galleries of the mine at Hallstatt, some of which existed as early as the end of the Bronze Age (that is, c. 10th–9th centuries BC), were dug into the side of the mountain following the veins of salt. With their numerous side passages they extend for more than 12,000 feet over an area of almost 330,000 square feet, and the largest reached a depth of about 700 feet. Similar construction techniques had already been used in the Bronze Age at the Mitterberg copper mines in Austria. Remains of many utensils in these galleries have been preserved by the salt: picks for cutting into the rock, knapsacks for carrying blocks of salt to the surface, wooden tubs for transporting food and water, and what may be torches or matches—long resinous sticks that miners may have held between their teeth to provide light while they worked in the galleries.

In the 6th century BC, from central France to Austria, the early Celts formed rich settlements run by unified dynasties. An original culture was forged, one that began to open up to the Mediterranean world. A taste for mead and wine from Greece or Etruria (modern Tuscany, in western Italy) inspired goldsmiths and other artisans, who celebrated their godlike warrior heroes.

CHAPTER II
THE FIRST CELTIC PRINCES

Whether as a dancing wrestler on a prince's bronze burial couch (opposite) or as a life-size sandstone statue (right) that topped a barrow found in Germany, the theme of the warrior-hero crops up in Celtic graves everywhere. The conical hat, gold collar, belt, and dagger are characteristic and are found in both symbolic representations and grave furnishings.

Around 600 BC the Phocaeans, Greeks who had originally settled in Asia Minor four centuries earlier, founded Massalia (now Marseilles) in southern France. This was to be a focal point for further coastal colonization. At the same time the first Celtic cultural center was developing deep within a broad expanse of western central Europe. Throughout the 6th century this Celtic center was conspicuous for its wealth, the dynamism of its culture, and its brilliant clan-based society ruled by powerful princes.

The Celts were already known to the Greeks. Hecataeus of Miletus, a geographer and writer from Asia Minor, mentioned the Celts by name for the first time in the 6th century BC as being neighbors of the Ligurians, implying that they were settled to the north of what is now Provence. In the next century Greek historian Herodotus (c. 484–c. 425) placed the Celts around the Danube River (which flows from southern Germany to the Black Sea)

and beyond the Pillars of Hercules at the east end of the Strait of Gibraltar.

The Hohenasperg citadel (left) in all its glory, dominating a vast landscape. At its foot several Celtic princes were buried under thirteen barrows within a radius of about 15 miles.

Rich Citadels North of the Alps

The birth of this new society was marked by the establishment of citadels, or fortresses, in high places overlooking vast tracts of land. A dozen of the most important of these places were probably residences of princes or territorial chiefs who played key roles not only in the economy and politics of

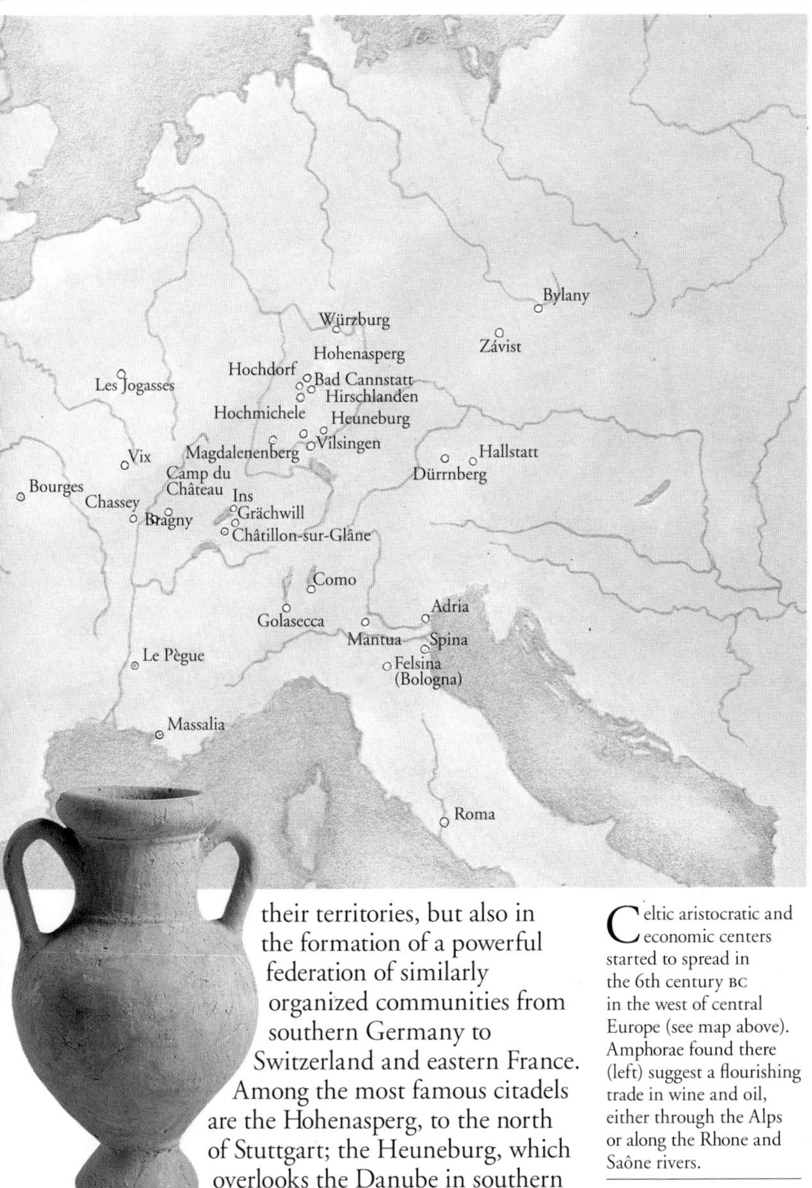

their territories, but also in the formation of a powerful federation of similarly organized communities from southern Germany to Switzerland and eastern France. Among the most famous citadels are the Hohenasperg, to the north of Stuttgart; the Heuneburg, which overlooks the Danube in southern

Celtic aristocratic and economic centers started to spread in the 6th century BC in the west of central Europe (see map above). Amphorae found there (left) suggest a flourishing trade in wine and oil, either through the Alps or along the Rhone and Saône rivers.

Germany; Uetliberg, in central Switzerland; Châtillon-sur-Glâne, in western Switzerland; and Mont Lassois, in eastern France, to name a few.

On level ground, other more recently discovered sites have yielded material exactly like that from the citadels, in particular, quantities of Mediterranean imports. These places may have been trading posts, as at Bragny-sur-Loire, in eastern central France, or other forms of princely settlement, as at Bourges, to the northwest, where several graves with imported bronze vessels were found during the 19th century.

Some aspects of this Early Iron Age civilization are spectacular: There was a new profusion of exotic products imported from the south, complex and solemn rites were conducted at funeral ceremonies, and there was a strong personal bias in dynastic power. These princes were the Celts' most important figures, yet little is known about their palaces, since none of the citadels excavated so far has yielded one. There are, however, a few hints. At the Wittnauerhorn citadel, in northern Switzerland, two central buildings, larger than the others, might have been the residences of rulers, while at the base of one of the barrows at Giessübel-Talhau, not far from the Heuneburg, the plan of what may have been a vast dwelling has been discovered.

This jar (below) from Grächwill, a site near Bern, Switzerland, was probably made at a Spartan colony in c. 570 BC and is thought to have held drink for funeral rites. At its neck a winged figure recalls ancient oriental symbols of fertility and immortality—as well as the Greek goddess Artemis.

The Heuneburg

The Heuneburg is the most extensively excavated citadel, and its fortifying wall presents some startling features. More than 13 feet high and made of sun-dried mud bricks

on a stone base, it was designed with projecting bastions, architecture wholly exceptional north of the Alps but well known in the Mediterranean world (in Sicily, for instance). Might this be the work of an expatriate Greek architect or of a Celt who had learned his trade south of the Alps? Inside the wall, houses were distributed along narrow streets. Outside, a cluster of buildings surrounded this acropolis. Many shards of black- and red-figure pottery mingled with Greek amphorae and Etruscan products. It seems there were brilliant local craftspeople. Not only did the Heuneburg potters have potters' wheels, but the metalsmiths were able to reproduce or repair

Built on a promontory above the Danube, the 6th-century BC Heuneburg fortress (plan, above left, and photograph of part of its wall, above right) was surrounded by eleven burial mounds within a 3-mile radius. Its square towers and nearly 2000 feet of mud-brick wall built on a stone base—a Mediterranean technique—raises questions about its architects and builders. So does the curious mold for a wine flagon handle piece (left) found there: Locally made, it has a satyr's head, a motif that the Etruscans also used on their flagons.

imported products, as shown by the clay mold for part of an Etruscan wine flagon handle found on the site. Does this represent the assimilation of techniques or the introduction of foreign workers?

A dead man's sacrificed wife might share his grave. The drawing below left is a reconstruction of a grave found in Germany based on the arrangement of the tomb when it was opened. The woman lay under the wagon's wheels, and the man beside them. The body of the wagon may have been taken off for the man to lie on.

Funerals Fit for Kings

The largest barrow of this period is the Magdalenenberg site in southern Germany's Black Forest, an area rich in iron ore. It is over 325 feet in diameter and must have attracted covetous attention, as it was robbed soon after the funeral. Dendrochronological analysis of the chamber walls dates the burial to 550 BC. The tomb was gutted in 504 BC, as evidenced by pieces of wooden tools abandoned there by their ghoulish owners.

Usually a barrow's central tomb belonged to a prince. This was a vast funerary chamber surrounded by secondary tombs—probably for relatives or family members—that continued to be used for generations.

Designed to move slowly and straight ahead, the funerary wagons of Celtic princes had fixed steering shafts (reconstruction below). Analysis of the wood from several wagons shows that different types were carefully selected for different parts.

The presence of a funerary wagon is the most original feature of these princely graves. Were the wagons used only for funerals or also for processions during a prince's lifetime? Curiously, the wheels of some wagons were taken off and arranged along the walls of the log-built tomb.

To the north of the Alps ritual carts or symbolic wheels had already been used for religious purposes for several generations. For a long time the models for these wagons were thought to have come from Italy. Yet the Celtic wagons are made differently. Their ritual wagons seem to have descended from ancient local Bronze Age beliefs. Sometimes accompanied by his wife, who had been killed as part of the funeral ritual, the dead man was adorned with personal ornaments and symbols of power.

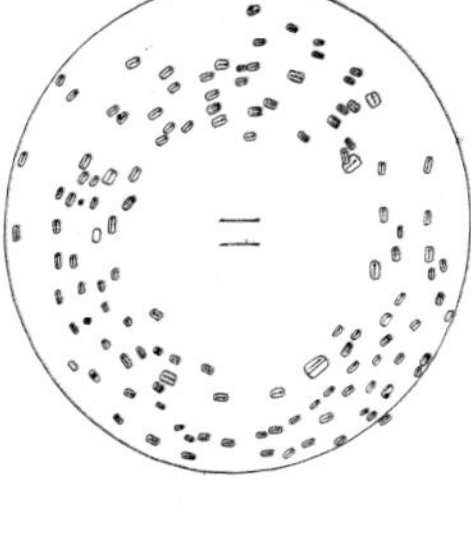

The Kaltbrunn barrow (top, in an 1864 painting) was excavated by the order of Grand Duke Frederick of Baden in 1864. Above is a typical plan of an Iron Age barrow, a sort of family or tribal vault. The prince's grave is in the center, and secondary graves were placed around it until another family or tribe rose to power and a different barrow was used.

The Hochdorf Prince

Painstaking excavation of a prince's tomb in the village of Hochdorf, a few miles from Stuttgart, has yielded invaluable information. The inside walls of the funerary chamber, built of oak logs, each measured about 15 feet. Cloths spread on the ground and draped on the walls were fixed in place with iron hooks and pinned together with fibulae. The prince, around forty years old, was tall for his period (about 6 feet) and was buried between 540 and 520 BC with especially rich offerings. He was lying not on a wagon but on a couch of sheet bronze that stood on little wheels. His clothing was secured by bronze and gold fibulae, and he wore a hat made of meticulously sewn birch bark. Around his neck, in addition to a gold collar, were amber

It has been noticed that many princely graves contained people who were of above-average height. The Hochdorf prince, too, was tall; his skull (below) was large, and his facial features broad and generous. Although the cause of his death at a rather advanced age for his time is not known, it seems likely that he suffered from arthritis. The prince's leather boots, which came up to his ankles and probably turned up at the toes, were covered in embossed gold leaf (above left) during the funeral ceremony.

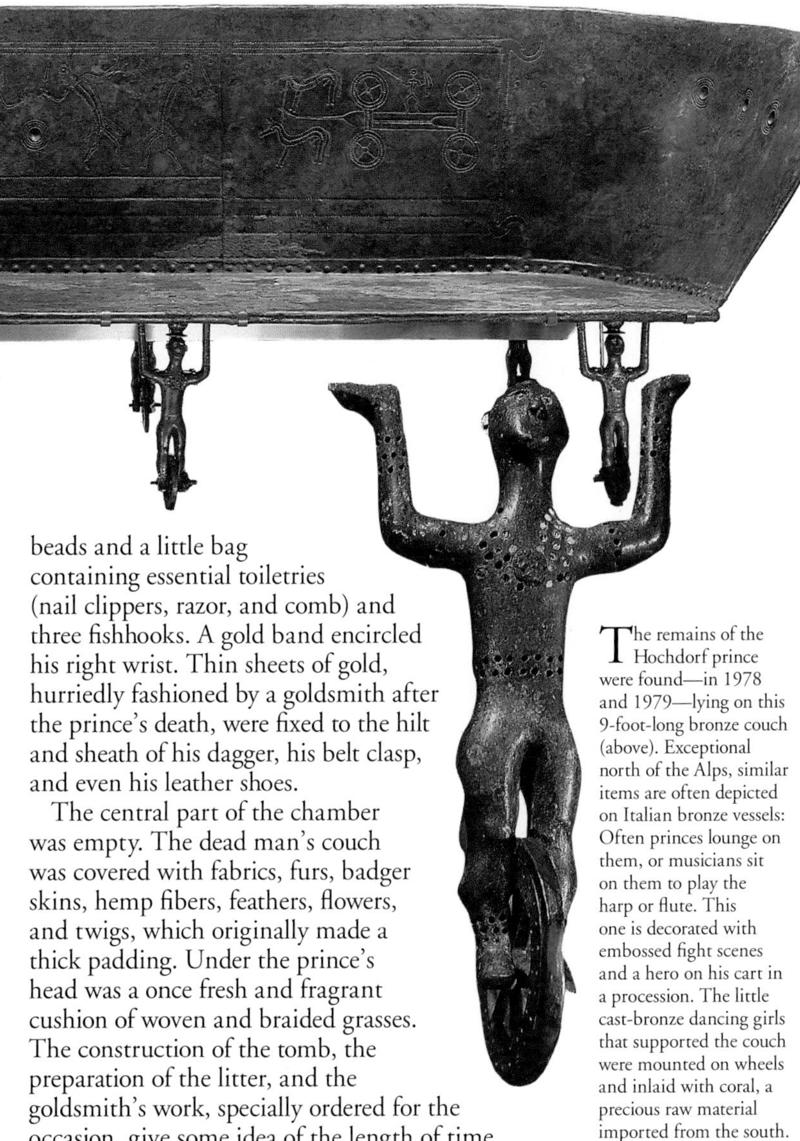

beads and a little bag containing essential toiletries (nail clippers, razor, and comb) and three fishhooks. A gold band encircled his right wrist. Thin sheets of gold, hurriedly fashioned by a goldsmith after the prince's death, were fixed to the hilt and sheath of his dagger, his belt clasp, and even his leather shoes.

The central part of the chamber was empty. The dead man's couch was covered with fabrics, furs, badger skins, hemp fibers, feathers, flowers, and twigs, which originally made a thick padding. Under the prince's head was a once fresh and fragrant cushion of woven and braided grasses. The construction of the tomb, the preparation of the litter, and the goldsmith's work, specially ordered for the occasion, give some idea of the length of time it took to prepare for such funeral ceremonies.

The remains of the Hochdorf prince were found—in 1978 and 1979—lying on this 9-foot-long bronze couch (above). Exceptional north of the Alps, similar items are often depicted on Italian bronze vessels: Often princes lounge on them, or musicians sit on them to play the harp or flute. This one is decorated with embossed fight scenes and a hero on his cart in a procession. The little cast-bronze dancing girls that supported the couch were mounted on wheels and inlaid with coral, a precious raw material imported from the south.

Drinking Horns and Mead

The large set of drinking equipment in the Hochdorf tomb included nine drinking horns hung along one wall. They were decorated for the occasion with strips of gold foil. The largest was an iron horn nearly 4 feet long and holding 5 quarts. At the prince's feet a bronze 125-gallon cauldron decorated with lion figurines stood on a wooden tripod. A golden cup used for dipping was balanced on its rim. The brownish remains in the bottom of the great cauldron have revealed that it was used for a serving of mead at the farewell feast. Pollen analysis suggests that the beverage was based on honey and spiced with local plants such as thyme, mountain jasmine, plantain, knapweed, and meadowsweet.

On the iron-trimmed wagon was laid a banquet service, complete with bronze bowls and plates. An ax, two knives, and an iron spearhead were also placed there, as were pieces of a horse's harness and a long wooden prod, or goad.

Sets of vessels for food and drink were usually put into the funerary chamber. Drinking horns, large bronze or pottery dishes, cauldrons, and buckets of native design were gradually replaced by wine-drinking wares—such as wine flagons or basins decorated with griffins' heads and standing on tripods (below)—imported from Greece, Etruria, or southern Italy. The Hochdorf prince's drinking horn (left) is exceptional both because of its size and because it is made of iron and gold rather than the usual animal horn.

The Symposium Ceremony

The Hochdorf cauldron, whose decorative lions came from Greek workshops, is one of the objects that demonstrate the existence of long-distance trade in ornamental goods with Mediterranean countries. The jar from Grächwill (see p. 32) and a large krater, or vase, from Vix, in France (see p. 42), are among the most famous imported drinking utensils used for "symposium" ceremonies. (An ancient ritual practiced both in the Hallstattian world and by the Greeks, a symposium was a banquet at which the dead man's

faithful companions assembled for the last time.) Many locally made bronze vessels have also been found at grave sites, especially at Hallstatt.

As the Hochdorf tomb (reconstruction above) remained intact until 1978, many observations could be made on the spot. Painstaking excavation and laboratory analyses have determined that mead was contained in the cauldron (below).

A Taste for Wine

New contacts with the south introduced the Celts to wine, a drink previously unknown north of the Alps and one that was to have important cultural repercussions. The Celts loved wine, and it soon became one of the mainsprings of trade

with the Mediterranean world. It was transported as a spiced concentrate in amphorae, plentiful remains of which are found in settlement sites. From 500 BC onward wine would replace the traditional mead at symposia: Traces of wine were discovered in the bottom of a bronze flask found in a prince's tomb in Hallein, Austria. Greek and Etruscan vessels, including the famous wine flagons, were refinements that went with wine drinking—and drunkenness—at princes' festivals and funeral meals.

Exceptional in shape and size (about 20 inches high), the prince of Hallein's flask (left) was mounted on legs and still contained traces of wine. The Etruscan wine flagon below is from the Lake Como area, in northern Italy.

Gold and Power

A golden torque was the supreme symbol of power. Made of sheets of beaten gold, these collars were usually decorated with small stamped geometric motifs, a legacy of Bronze Age abstract art. They are found on all the chiefs buried in the richest wagon graves. These men were armed with daggers and commonly sported gold bracelets on their right arms. They were often also buried with a gold cup resting on the rim of the vessel that contained the drink. Unlike these luxury items, which were probably used while the princes, or chieftains, were alive, some objects placed in their graves were covered in gold only during the funeral rites. The goldsmith must have worked close to the barrow, using a set of small stamps whose identical impressions can be found as a form of identification on various different items.

Even in the richest women's graves—those of princes' wives or members of their family—gold is not as evident; it is used only to decorate the women's hair. They wore large spherical gold pins or loops that held veils around their faces.

Gold was strongly associated with the Celts' sense of identity. Native gold products held such deep meaning for the Celts that they felt no need to import other jewelry. The influence of Mediterranean goldsmiths' work can be traced only in the sporadic adoption of techniques like soldering and filigree, both used to perfection by Celtic goldsmiths.

The large bead and pendant below, found near Bern, are similar to Etruscan products.

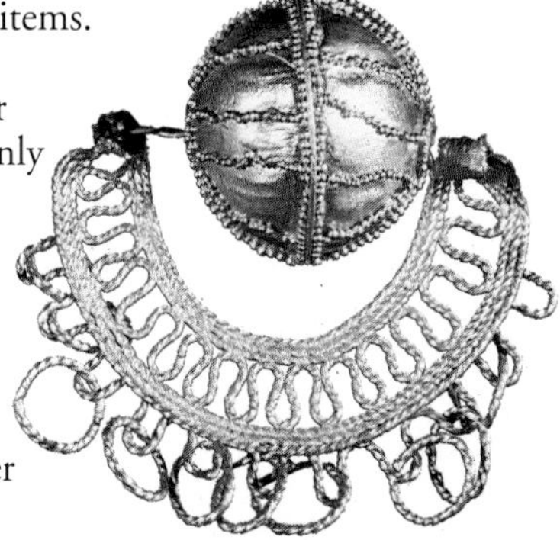

A prince's gold torque (below) recalls the abstract art of the Bronze Age. High-ranking women wore bracelets, beads, large-headed pins, and earrings of hammered and embossed gold leaf (opposite).

The Extravagant Princess of Vix

The most extraordinary Celtic tomb discovered in France in the 20th century belonged to a woman about thirty-five years of age who died around 480 BC. This woman—known as the princess of Vix—was undoubtedly as powerful as any of the greatest princes of her time. She was found near Mont Lassois, in eastern France, lying on a small wagon whose wheels had been removed. Beside the wagon was an enormous bronze krater—probably from southern Italy—with a large lid. Several other vessels had been placed on its rim: a silver cup with a gilded ornamented boss, or stud, protected by a fiber

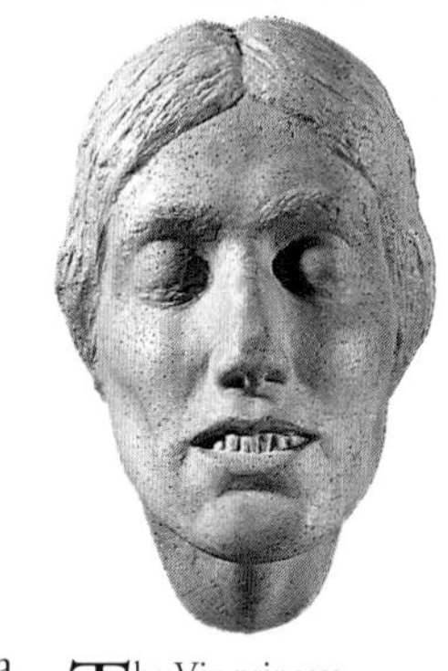

The Vix princess seems to have died at the age of about thirty-five. Her features were reconstructed from her skull and jawbone.

This, the largest known krater of antiquity (left), is from Vix, stands well over 5 feet high, weighs about 450 pounds, and holds almost 250 gallons. It was used to mix concentrated wine with water. A strainer filtered out the herbs and spices that flavored the wine. On its rim stood, among other things, a Greek cup (below) for sampling the result.

covering; two Greek cups; and a bronze Etruscan wine flagon. Along one wall were some Etruscan bowls that bear a striking resemblance to ones depicted in frescoes at Tarquinia, in central Italy. On the ground were blue and red pigments that probably came from cloths or decorative paintings.

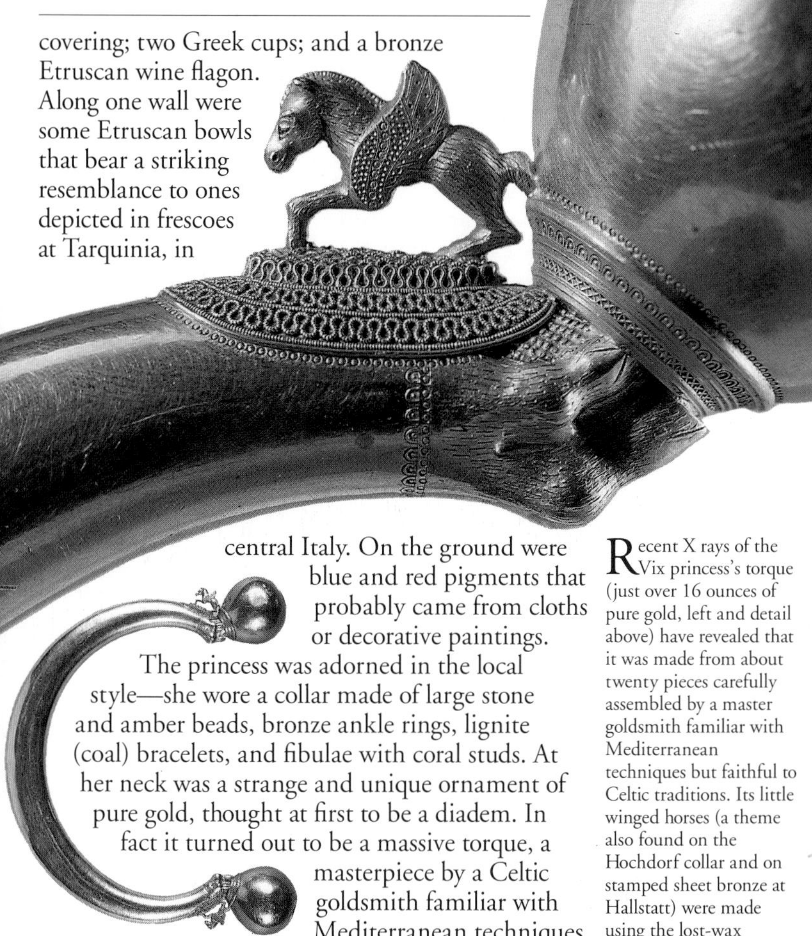

The princess was adorned in the local style—she wore a collar made of large stone and amber beads, bronze ankle rings, lignite (coal) bracelets, and fibulae with coral studs. At her neck was a strange and unique ornament of pure gold, thought at first to be a diadem. In fact it turned out to be a massive torque, a masterpiece by a Celtic goldsmith familiar with Mediterranean techniques. This attraction for things from the south is typical of this period, when Celtic artisans would often imitate all kinds of articles.

Recent X rays of the Vix princess's torque (just over 16 ounces of pure gold, left and detail above) have revealed that it was made from about twenty pieces carefully assembled by a master goldsmith familiar with Mediterranean techniques but faithful to Celtic traditions. Its little winged horses (a theme also found on the Hochdorf collar and on stamped sheet bronze at Hallstatt) were made using the lost-wax process. The filigree and beaded threads they stand on are only 0.2 millimeters thick. The round terminals are attached to the collar by rings bearing a stamped decoration of local design.

Trade Among Equals

Skilled crafts developed in the Alpine salt- and copper-mining areas. Iron ore, which is widely distributed geographically, was exploited fairly early on, especially in areas like central and northeastern

France, which played a major role in shaping the culture of the Early Iron Age. There is no surviving material evidence for the techniques of iron extraction or forging used at that time, but it is clear that blacksmiths were already able to make wheel hoops and wagon trappings. Bronzeworking was now restricted to personal ornaments and tableware. Potters were less prestigious. For the most part their products were shaped by hand and were colorfully decorated with red hematite, white chalk, or glossy black graphite. The rarer imported raw materials—such as amber, lignite, coral, and ivory—were worked by specialized artisans attached to princely courts.

The early Celtic centers, with their marked hierarchical organization, were essentially nodal points on long-range trading networks that led through the Alpine passes or along the Rhone River in France and Switzerland. Their choice of imports was selective: The Celts would not let Greek and Etruscan merchants dictate to them but decided for themselves which goods they needed to satisfy their taste in luxuries or which goods fit in with traditional regional rituals that had been handed down from

Metalworkers ranked highest of all artisans: First came the blacksmiths, then bronzesmiths, coppersmiths, and metal casters. There is little evidence for techniques of iron extraction or for the workshops themselves, but smiths were certainly able to make wheel hoops and cart trappings. Bronzesmiths specialized in making personal ornaments and utensils.

This bronze bucket covered with several layers of cloth served as a receptacle for the ashes of a cremation burial. A rite that involved covering the grave goods in fabric has often been observed and probably indicates an ultimate concern for preserving the dead person's possessions.

Specialized artisans attached to a prince's court worked imported raw materials—amber, lignite, coral, and ivory. The glass industry was also on the rise.

Glass beads from Slovenia (left), an area adjoining the eastern Celtic zone. Where the Halstattian world was in contact with the Adriatic area, women were very fond of eye motifs and colors that brightened up their finery.

Bronze Age times. The colonial model that used to be invoked has now been abandoned: Greeks and Etruscans clearly dealt with the Celts as equals. The latter, after all, had ample to export in return—salt, tin, copper, wool, hides, furs, and gold.

Amber from the Baltic was the raw material for many Celtic necklaces (above).

The wide belts of sheet bronze worn by the first Celts (left) were stamped with repetitive geometric motifs like those later used on princes' collars.

Traditional Style in the Illyrian Vein

The Early Iron Age Celts are divided into two geographical groups: the western zone, where swords were worn, and the eastern zone, where axes were carried. The same division applies to the artistic sphere, especially in the decoration of objects like pottery, whose overall shape is otherwise similar. In the western zone abstract art of Bronze Age ancestry prevails, while the eastern zone tended toward a more narrative style.

Already in the 7th century BC urns from central Europe were displaying schematic silhouettes of dancers, musicians, weavers, women with raised arms, and warriors. On vessels of hammered bronze from a cemetery in eastern Austria this figurative trend —depictions of processions of people and mythical hunting scenes—blends with the geometric tradition. One of the graves even included a human

The stag and the wild boar were favorite Celtic beasts. Along with other figurines of animals or warrior-heroes, this tiny bronze boar (left), measuring about 2 inches, was a votive offering found at the sanctuary of Balzers (Liechtenstein).

This 7th-century BC Bavarian pot has figures of people or animals pricked into the clay, still in a rigid geometric style.

This small (roughly 19 inches) wagon from Strettweg, Austria, brings together many Celtic sacred images. A nature goddess bearing an incense burner is surrounded by mounted warriors and men holding stags by their antlers.

mask and severed hands made of sheet bronze that showed the influence of the Illyrian world to the south. Funerary masks of the same period made of gold foil have been found in Macedonia (in the former Yugoslavia).

Similar figures with obvious mythological significance—including a large goddess, warriors, and animals (in this case stags, but sometimes wild boars)—form a scene on the wagon placed in a cremation grave at Strettweg, a site in Austria.

Master bronzesmiths north of the Alps carried on the art of situla decoration and illustrated familiar heroic entertainments. Shown on this situla (left) from Kuffarn, Austria, is a prince in a wide-brimmed hat holding out his cup to a servant pouring wine while, behind him, a companion goes to refill two empty containers.

Situla Art

A taste for depicting narrative scenes on vessels or belt clasps goes back to the 7th century BC and started in Etruria. Designs enlivened by griffins, sphinxes, lions, grazing stags, and various plant motifs spread toward the Adriatic Sea, where they developed into a form called situla art (usually decorated bronze buckets). One of the earliest examples, dated c. 650 BC, was

Situlae were buckets made of hammered sheet bronze with curved rims and sometimes lids (drawing above). Situla art originated in the Adriatic, Etruria, and Slovenia and then spread to the eastern Alps.

In 6th- and 5th-century BC Slovenia, decorated bronze plaques ornamented the wide belts of men of high rank. One from Magdalenska Gora, in Slovenia, shows a horseman and boxers with dumbbells (above left). The boxers face one another on either side of a plumed helmet that seems to belong to the symbolic world of Iron Age warriors; examples are also sometimes found at sites in the Alps. A detail from a belt plaque from Vače, also in Slovenia, shows a foot soldier wearing the same type of helmet and bearing a shield, an ax, and two lances (left).

found in Este, in northern Italy, although the workshops that specialized in making these situlae were confined to northern Slovenia, in the former Yugoslavia. With their stunning mastery of repoussé (relief) work and chasing, the bronzesmiths portrayed scenes from the heavenly afterlife that lay in store for warrior-heroes: feasts, processions, hunts, spectacles of games and fights, and other pleasures, with women shown taking the role of servants. Situla art played an important part in the genesis of Celtic art. The theme of the deified hero, dear to the Celts, put in its next appearance on the fringe of the western zone, at Hirschlanden and Hochdorf, in southern Germany.

Fearless Celtic warriors, renowned for their courage, first seized Rome and then launched an assault on Delphi, in central Greece. But the period of conquests lasted less than a century. The Celts never achieved a truly centralized power or empire in the political sense of the word, yet they left a lasting mark upon the different peoples they encountered.

CHAPTER III
THE ALL-CONQUERING CELTS

Very gradually the water bird motifs of the Bronze Age gave way to doves and then birds of prey (a fibula from Dürrnberg, a site near Hallein, in Austria, right). Images of the Celts reflect their increasing aggression and lust for wealth. Opposite: Detail from the 2nd-century BC Roman Civitalba frieze commemorating Rome's victory over the Celts.

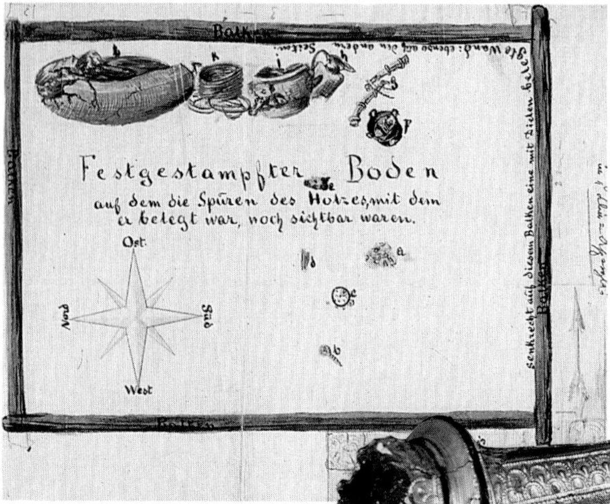

Near the Hohenasperg a burial was made at a site known as Kleinaspergle in about 450 BC (recorded in a watercolor, left). It recalled its predecessors' splendor in imported wares—an Etruscan wine jar and two Greek cups—but also displayed symbols of the new type of power. These were a local copy of a bronze wine flagon, two gold-plated drinking horns, a cordon cist (a ribbed bronze bucket), a large bronze bowl, and a belt clasp decorated with gold and coral.

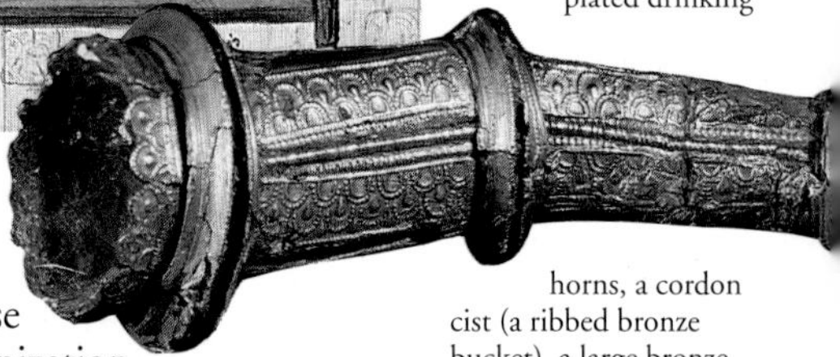

The ram, symbolic of strength, was often used as an ornamental theme in Celtic art. A ram's head formed the tip of this mid-5th-century Kleinaspergle drinking horn, whose mount (above) is almost 7 inches long and made of iron, bronze, and gold.

The power of the Early Iron Age princes crumbled after two or three generations. Whether because of an internal crisis, a reorganization of trading networks, or a conflict between Greeks and Etruscans for control of trade, the Celtic centers of commercial relations were abandoned around 500 BC in favor of a more rural way of life, now governed by warrior chieftains.

A few of the old centers, including the Hohenasperg, held out for a little longer, but all eventually collapsed. On their margins, during the 5th century, new regions became the focal points of civilization: the Rhineland (the area west of the Rhine, in Germany); Bohemia; and the regions of Champagne and Ardennes (in northeastern France).

Social Leveling

Customs and material culture slowly reflected these societal changes. Luxury items found in graves of this period suggest that the social distance had lessened between those in positions of relative power and the rest of the people. Mediterranean imports dropped off, and jewelry became less sumptuous. Chiefs' graves lost their monumental character and lavish show of wealth, though they still retained a wide range of goods.

While the Late Iron Age seems to have been a more democratic period, it was also more warlike. The ceremonial dagger, symbol of power for the early Celts, gave way to the complete armor of the warrior. Princes, or rather warrior-aristocrats like the lord of Hallein, were buried on two-wheeled chariots—fighting vehicles designed for speed—and no longer on ceremonial wagons.

Following Etruscan custom, mirrors became essential accessories for women of the 5th-century Celtic aristocracy, who took them to their graves. Above: A mirror from La Motte-St.-Valentin, in northeastern France.

The Cradles of Celtic Art

From the end of the 6th until the middle of the 4th century BC a small group of Celts in the Hunsrück and Eifel hills, on the west bank of the Rhine river in the westernmost part of Germany, stood out particularly in terms of both their dynamism and their conservatism.

These Celts had the greatest concentration of rich graves of that period. The graves were placed under barrows, often in groups, and were sometimes related to defended settlements. Several aristocratic persons

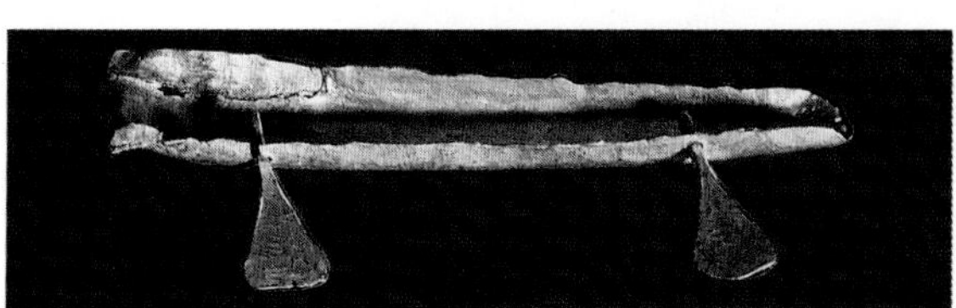

With two oars and an upturned prow, this miniature gold boat (less than 3 inches long) came from a warrior's grave in Austria. It has the traditional shape of vessels that in the Iron Age carried salt, among other things, and today still ply the lakes of the Salzkammergut region.

were buried there in rites typical of the early Celts northwest of the Alps, with torques, bracelets, fibulae, and belt and chariot fittings in bronze or iron, and gold mounts on drinking vessels—all decorated in the early Celtic style.

A bronze or, especially, a gold bracelet, sometimes lavishly decorated, would for a long time remain a mark of nobility for one category of high-ranking warrior. A small number, including that of the chief of Kleinaspergle, were trimmed with iron or gold-plated bronze and coral studs.

Further east, in Bohemia, a similar civilization blossomed. Defended villages were built or rebuilt. The Celtic chieftains of Bohemia sported the same personal adornments as their Rhineland cousins.

The Schwarzenbach tomb contained a small sheet-gold face (below) and a fine openwork gold mount (bottom left) that probably once encased a wooden bowl.

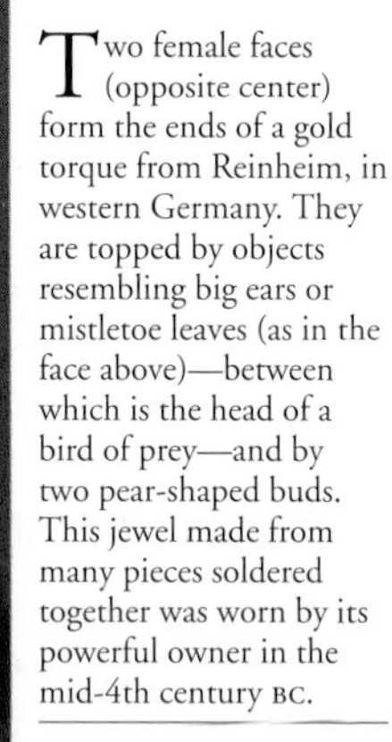

Two female faces (opposite center) form the ends of a gold torque from Reinheim, in western Germany. They are topped by objects resembling big ears or mistletoe leaves (as in the face above)—between which is the head of a bird of prey—and by two pear-shaped buds. This jewel made from many pieces soldered together was worn by its powerful owner in the mid-4th century BC.

Between the Saar River in France and the Rhineland it is common for rich barrow graves to contain drinking wares embellished with precious metal: drinking horns fitted with gold mounts and lids, or wooden cups covered in gold tracery.

Exceptional Women

The women who lived in this region were given distinguished burials, and a few graves have spectacular furnishings: one at Bad Dürkheim—containing an Etruscan tripod and wine jar and a golden torque and bracelet—and two others belonging to the princesses of Reinheim and Waldalgesheim, who lived at the beginning and end of the 4th century BC, respectively. All the women discovered surrounded by objects bespeaking rank must, like the princess of Vix, have played a part equal to that of the greatest Celtic chiefs.

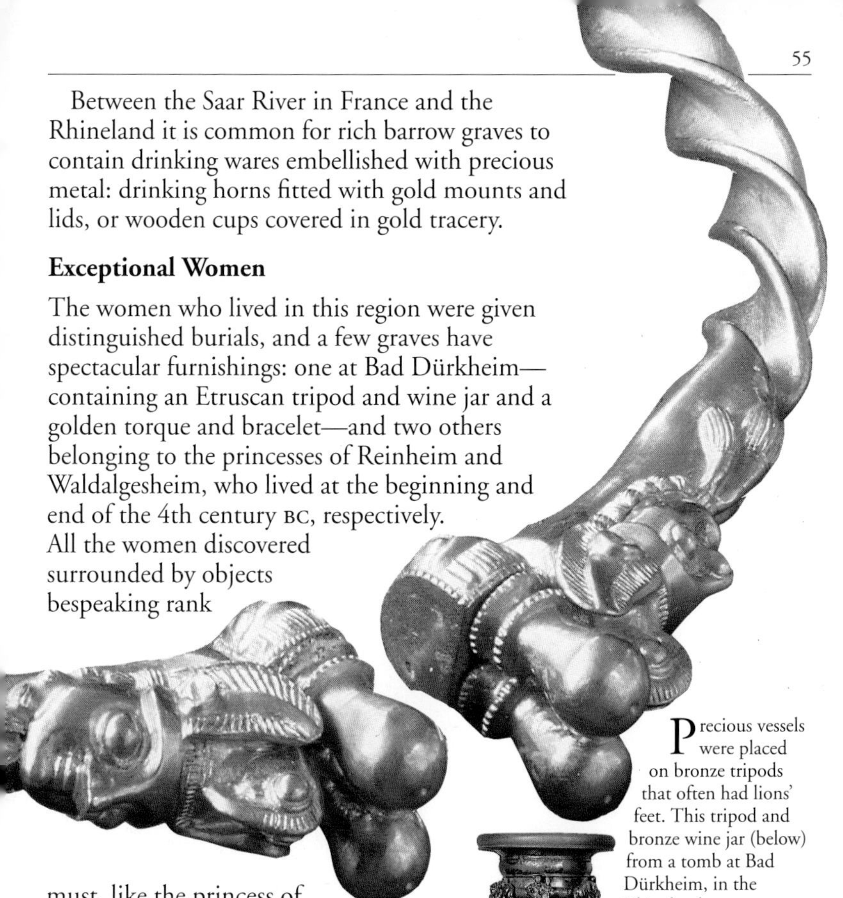

Precious vessels were placed on bronze tripods that often had lions' feet. This tripod and bronze wine jar (below) from a tomb at Bad Dürkheim, in the Rhineland, were imported from Etruria in the 5th century BC.

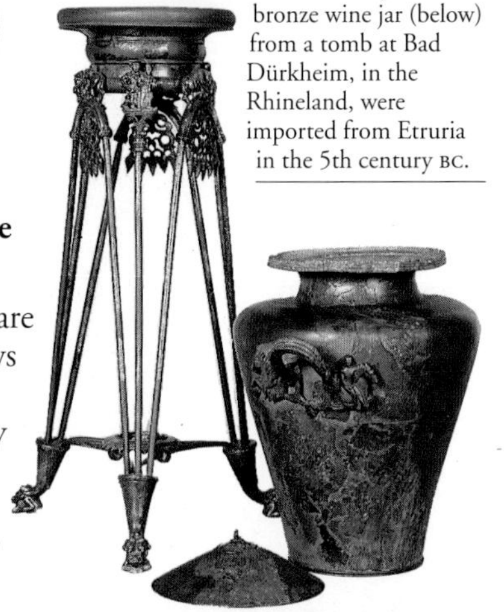

The Nonconformism of Champagne

The vast Late Iron Age cemeteries of Champagne, in northeastern France, are made up of flat graves without barrows (a sign of a dense population), which are dug deep into the chalky soil. Easy to find, these sites began to be excavated in the 19th century, but often only sketchily. The pottery they

contained is of regional "Marnian" (from the Marne River) style, but Etruscan wine flagons from a few of the sites show contact between Champagne and Etruria.

The most important men of this region were buried on their chariots. (There are more than 150 of these, but this is only a small proportion of all the Celtic graves there.) These men were usually armed and wore bronze helmets. The decorative parts of their horses' harnesses were placed in their graves. Infantry warriors had only their armaments: swords, spears, and javelins. Women had belt clasps, fibulae to pin their clothes, and other symbolic jewelry, such as torques.

The 5th and early 4th centuries BC were a time of great stability, and this was reflected in material goods. The society was fairly egalitarian, though the fact that there are more women's graves may be due to the departure of men for other horizons.

Typical of work in 5th-century BC northeastern France, a large vase (left) is decorated with monstrous incised eels. Pointed helmets, like the one below from the early 4th century BC, were among the arms buried with princes on their two-wheeled war chariots.

A Unique Style

In the 5th century BC technical innovations allowed the Celts to break away from the repetitive

Phalerae were disks, usually made of bronze, that decorated horses' harnesses or chariots. This one from Cuperly, in the Marne region of France, was 4 inches in diameter and came from the grave of a rich warrior buried in the late 5th or early 4th century BC (left). It is made of a number of different pieces, notably openwork bosses in relief. The perfect arrangement suggests that it was designed using a compass. Simpler, but also larger, are the phalerae from nearby St.-Jean-sur-Tourbe, which are nearly 10 inches in diameter (below).

geometric art that had been in vogue in many areas during the Early Iron Age. Lines began to flow more freely, and the assimilation of Mediterranean influences reached perfection.

Oriental themes were introduced: the tree of life surrounded by birds, dragons, palmettes, lotus flowers, and human masks. Found from Champagne to Bohemia and the Carpathians, these motifs hint at profound changes in belief systems and form new magical symbols that would remain a part of Celtic artists' repertoire for centuries to come.

The introduction of drypoint compasses allowed complex new patterns to be made. A marked taste for ambiguity and the interplay of lines and shapes at the expense of natural forms—a taste that perhaps echoed other trends in Celtic thought—became fundamental elements in the decorative art that embellished the treasures of the elite.

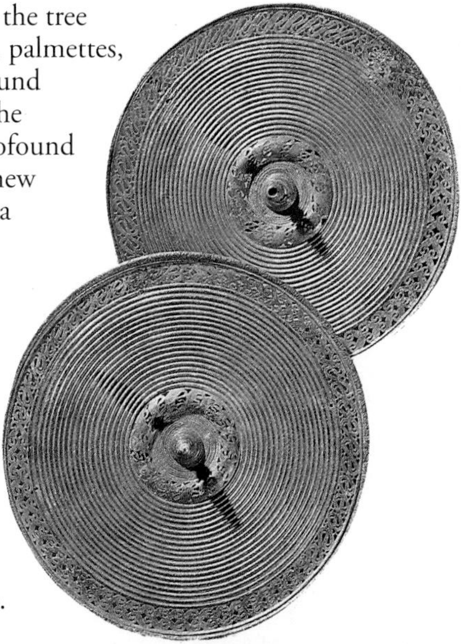

Regional Imagery

These widely shared themes varied in regional interpretation. Fibulae with symmetrical double masks were produced mainly in the middle Rhineland, while ones with asymmetrical bows were made mostly in the east. The wild boar, a bird in flight, or fibulae shaped like shoes came from the Dürrnberg workshops in Austria. Fantastic figurative designs were most common in Bohemia but were relatively rare in Switzerland and Champagne, areas that showed less exuberant taste.

These imaginative figure designs (in the 5th and early 4th centuries BC) were also adapted to pottery. In Champagne and the Ardennes wheel-turned pedestal vases were painted in bold red curvilinear designs. In Armorica (now Brittany) black pottery mimicked the shapes of metal vessels and was decorated with stamped motifs or incised designs based on the palmette.

On this pedestal vase (left) from Prunay, a site near the Marne River, the curving design was made using a slip (a clay coating rich in metallic oxides) that produces contrasting red and black when fired.

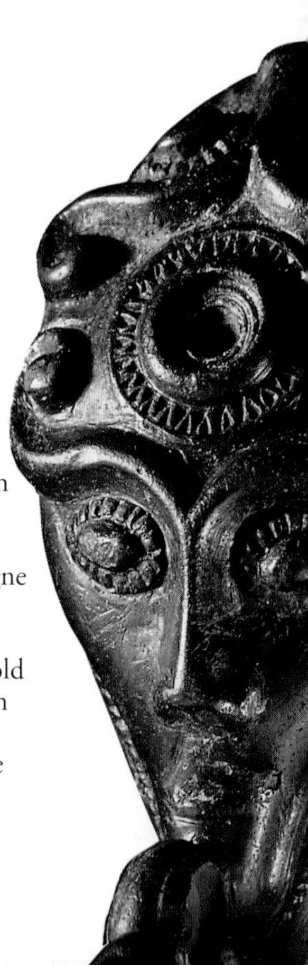

The Urge to Migrate

According to legend, the Celts of Gaul—the ancient name for the region to the south and west of the Rhine, west of the Alps, and north of the Pyrenees—at this time were under the rule of a tribe called the Bituriges and their king, Ambigatus. Anxious to relieve his kingdom of excess population, he decided to send his nephews Bellovesus and Segovesus, enterprising young men, to make new homes in whatever direction the gods chose. The oracle allotted the German Hercynian forest to Segovesus and Italy to Bellovesus. In reality, at the end of the 5th century BC some Celtic chiefs did embark upon a process of conquest of all the middle latitudes of Europe, followed by Mediterranean Europe as well. The Celts' fascination with Italy—and the confused situation into which Italy had fallen as Etruscan power declined—marked it as a prime target for invasion. Starting from north of the Alps, bands of Celts streamed into the peninsula. The newcomers' tracks can easily be traced: Objects such as belt clasps indicate that Celtic warriors were present in Languedoc in the 5th century BC, en route to Italy, into which they filtered gradually as scouts or as mercenaries seeking employment.

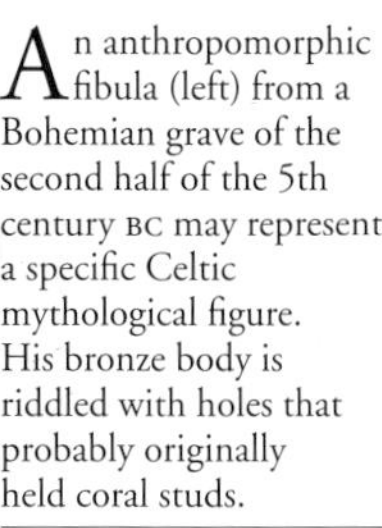

An anthropomorphic fibula (left) from a Bohemian grave of the second half of the 5th century BC may represent a specific Celtic mythological figure. His bronze body is riddled with holes that probably originally held coral studs.

The faces opposite and center are two parts of a single late-5th-century BC Slovakian fibula. This type of triple human mask was widespread, especially in central Europe. Two masks face each other, their chins on the bow of the brooch; a third is joined at the forehead to the larger face, where there is also a setting for a missing stud, probably of coral. Perfect examples of classical Celtic art, these faces boast eyebrows that swirl back from the nose to the top of the brow.

Assimilation of new motifs by the Transalpine Celts—those who lived in what is now France—and the important role of northern Italy in the transformation of Celtic art can be traced through openwork belt clasps. This one from Bavaria (left) uses the oriental theme of the tree of life.

A Host of Strange Creatures

At the beginning of the Late Iron Age a whole bestiary, including horses, wild boars, and birds, decorated small objects. Fibulae and other ornaments were decorated with human heads, animals, or fantastic creatures whose makeup sheds light on the Celts' symbolic system. On human faces the mouths and eyebrows are accentuated, while eyes and cheeks protrude; hair and beards take vegetal form; ears become pointed. Shown here, starting at the far left, are two 5th-century BC fibulae from the Hallein area—one with a donkey's head at one end and a grotesque human head at the other, and one in the form of a bird with a hooked beak; a piece of a wine flagon handle from Kleinaspergle with a half-human, half-bestial face; a sumptuous human-headed horse from the lid of a Reinheim flagon; a detail from the gold bracelet of a warrior; a decorative 4th-century BC harness buckle with two facing flamingos from the tomb of the Waldalgesheim princess; and a 2nd-century BC cast-bronze harness ring with a sleepy face.

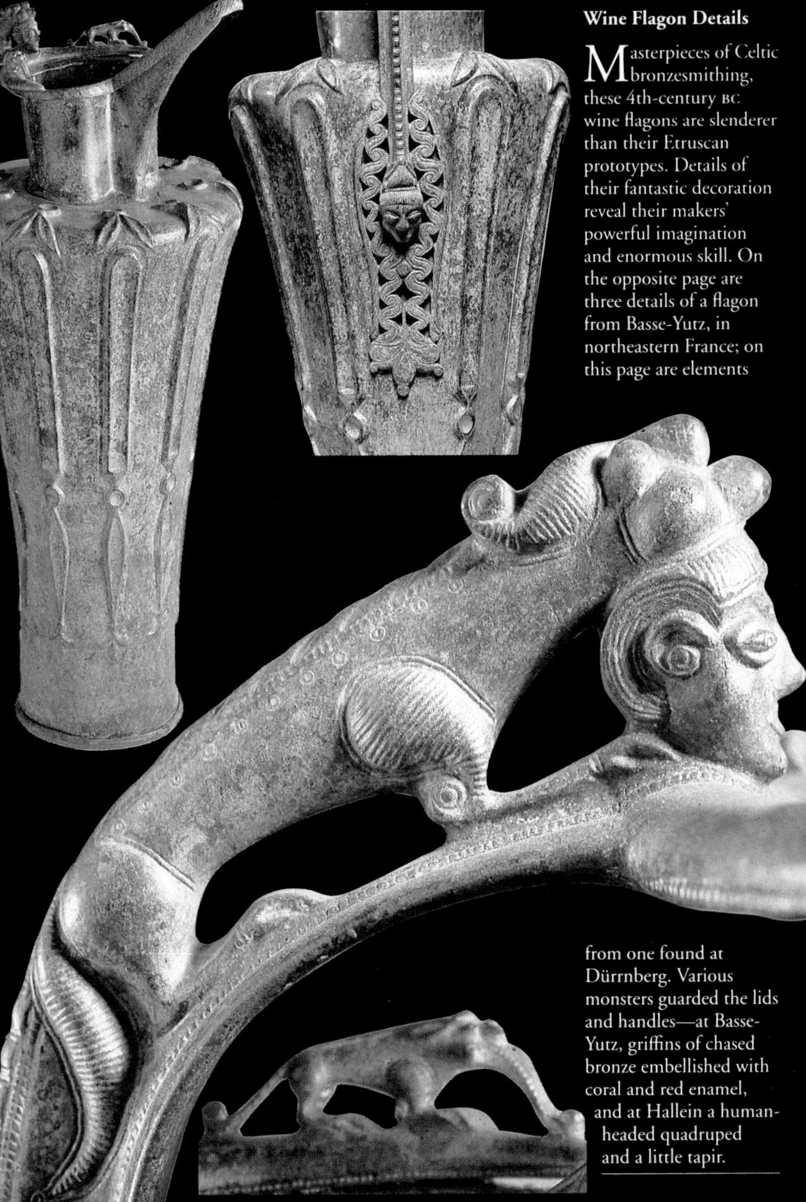

Wine Flagon Details

Masterpieces of Celtic bronzesmithing, these 4th-century BC wine flagons are slenderer than their Etruscan prototypes. Details of their fantastic decoration reveal their makers' powerful imagination and enormous skill. On the opposite page are three details of a flagon from Basse-Yutz, in northeastern France; on this page are elements from one found at Dürrnberg. Various monsters guarded the lids and handles—at Basse-Yutz, griffins of chased bronze embellished with coral and red enamel, and at Hallein a human-headed quadruped and a little tapir.

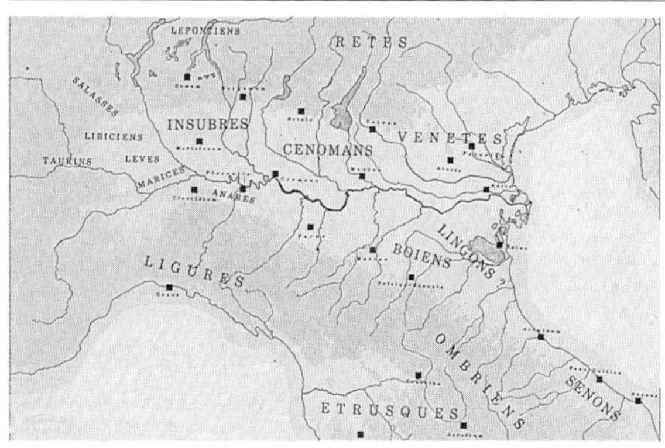

Celtic tribes in Italy: the Insubres at the foot of the Alps, with their capital at Mediolanum (now Milan); the Cenomani around Verona and in the Po Valley, with their capital at Brixia (now Brescia); the Boii around Parma and Bologna; and the Lingones on the Adriatic coast. The Senones were last to arrive in Italy.

The Celts Invaded Italy

Conquests began in earnest at the beginning of the 4th century BC: 300,000 Celts were on the move in a sort of *ver sacrum* (as described by ancient authors, this was a ritual exodus in which part of the population was chosen for foreign colonization).

Relations with other peoples shifted from the commercial and peaceful to the political and warlike, (although the actual situation was probably more complex). While ancient texts mainly describe wars between the Celts and the Romans or the way Celtic mercenaries profited from Mediterranean cities' internal conflicts, archaeological evidence presents a different picture, one in which the new arrivals fitted easily into Italian life—Celtic and Italian culture meeting in a true symbiosis.

This helmet (below) from Canosa di Puglia proves that Celts were present in southern Italy between 367 and 349 BC.

The Eternal City in the Hands of the Celts

The first wave of Celtic immigrants settled a substantial area of the Po River valley in Italy. Expansion southward began in about 400 BC, when Celts laid siege to the ancient Etruscan town of Clusium (now Chiusi), in central Italy. Next the Senones, a Celtic people from the Yonne River basin in central France, marched on Rome. The succeeding few years were marred by a series of tragic events: a Roman defeat a few miles from the city at the confluence of the Allia and Tiber rivers, then the destruction of Rome itself—it was sacked, burned down, and occupied for seven months.

The Celts laid siege to Rome and would have destroyed the Capitol, had watchful geese not alerted the Romans to the invaders. Warriors swept into every part of the city where they thought there might be rich spoils. They spared the Romans no shame and set a ransom of 1000 pounds of gold. Furthermore, the Celts tried to cheat the Romans by using loaded weights to measure out the gold, and when a

The Celts' adventure in Rome made a lasting impression on artists. Above: *The Gauls in Sight of Rome,* by Evariste Luminais. Below: A stele from Bormio, in northern Italy, an area where inscriptions in a Celtic language and alphabet first appeared in the 4th century BC.

Two paintings by a 19th-century artist.

"They were almost more hesitant to enter the open [mansions] than to break into the others: They felt a sort of awe in seeing, seated in their courtyards, those figures whose costumes lent them a superhuman grandeur.... The Gauls stood frozen before the Romans as before statues in a temple, until one of them, a certain Marcus Papirius, whose beard a warrior had touched... hit him over the head with his ivory staff. This unleashed his assailant's anger, and Papirius was killed with all the others, still in their seats.... The Gauls looted the houses and, after looting them, set them on fire."

Livy
(59 BC–AD 17)
History of Rome

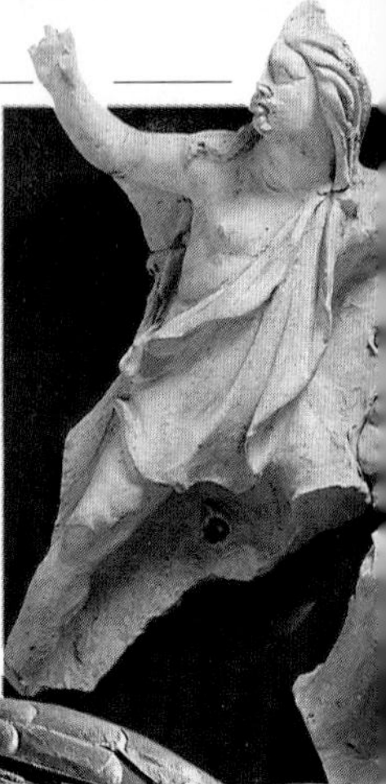

tribune complained, Brennus, the conquering hero, added his sword to the weights on the scales with the cynical words, "Woe to the defeated."

The Start of a Terrible Revenge

Soon after the Senones invaded Rome, ancient texts begin mentioning Celtic mercenaries as being involved in a whole series of Mediterranean conflicts. It seems that the Celts' Italian campaigns had been conducted with an exact foreknowledge of local conditions. Mercenary service was probably an early means by which they acquired such familiarity.

Many Transalpine Celts went on to organize raids in Apulia, Campania, and Etruria, regions in central and southern Italy. In 385 BC Celts helped tyrant Dionysius I of Syracuse, Sicily, to reduce the Etruscans' power and lead a campaign against the city of Caere (modern-day Cerveteri); their alliance with Dionysius lasted about thirty years. In 332 BC the Senones and Rome made peace. Then a fresh coalition was formed to break Rome's renewed expansion: The Senones, Etruscans, and Umbrians united, but were finally defeated at Sentinum, in Umbria, in 295 BC.

Suppression of the Celts then began. The Senones were conclusively beaten by Rome in 283 BC, and their lands were redistributed. In 249 there was another crisis; the Boii (originally from Bohemia) appealed for help to the Transalpine Celts, but together they were defeated in a terrible battle in 225 BC near Telamon, in Etruria. This

The Civitalba frieze was carved in the early 2nd century BC to commemorate Rome's victory over the invading Celts. Above, in the center, a Celt on his chariot knocks down one of his companions as he flees; behind him another defends himself from the pursuing Romans. Below: A bust of Alexander the Great by Lysippus (4th century BC). Opposite: A 3rd-century helmet from Çiumesti, in Romania.

war finally ended in 222 BC after the Romans captured Mediolanum (modern-day Milan), capital of the Celtic Insubres tribe. In 191 BC it was the turn of the Boii; they, too, submitted once and for all to Rome.

Boasting to Alexander the Great

Other Celts, led by Ambigatus's nephew Segovesus, had headed toward central Europe and the Balkans. Some probably reached Pannonia (now Hungary) near the end of the 5th century BC. The excavation of cemeteries in Slovakia has produced the characteristic belt clasps, swords, and knives.

One Celtic delegation met Alexander the Great, ruler of the Macedonian empire, in 335 BC somewhere near Bratislava, where the Morava River flows into the Danube, and they exchanged diplomatic gifts. Alexander asked the delegates what they most feared among men, hoping his own fame had reached Celtic lands and inspired fear and respect. Their reply surprised him: The Celts said they feared nothing except that the sky might one day fall in on them. Alexander called them friends, made them allies, and then dismissed them, commenting that they were braggarts.

A drinking horn found in the Eigenbilzen tomb had a decorative openwork mount (above). The strip of palmettes and the floral motif are typical of the flowing vegetal style.

The Waldalgesheim Style

Contact with the Etruscans and Greeks became more direct in the 4th century BC. Celtic artists—starting in Celto-Italic workshops—assimilated Mediterranean elements and went on to develop in a new direction, creating a flowing technique still called the Waldalgesheim style, after jewelry of this type found in a rich Rhineland grave. It is based on foliage and palmettes worked into continuous repetitive chainlike compositions in which static and dynamic elements alternate. At times these vegetal motifs seem to transform fleetingly into human faces.

Of Celtic remains in Italy, the southernmost find so far is a ceremonial helmet (see p. 64) with this type of decoration from Canosa di Puglia, a site located on Italy's "heel." The golden torque from Santa Paolina di Filottrano, another site on the Adriatic, found in one of the cemeteries of the Senones, illustrates this typically Celtic integration of Mediterranean motifs. The new style quickly spread north of the Alps and even into western France, where finds of ceremonial helmets and other ornaments prove this was a period of general Celtic expansion. An iron helmet from Agris, in western France, plated in bronze and completely covered in pure gold, is a masterpiece of 4th-century Celtic goldsmithing.

Meanwhile, the Cisalpine Celts in the Po River valley kept a firm hold on trade in coral, a treasure from the Bay of Naples. This trade began in the 6th century BC and was tied to the production of torques, helmets, and sword scabbards.

A harness ring from the Paris area. This ring and others found on routes taken during the Celts' long-range expeditions show human heads emerging from spiral designs.

The Danubian Style

Techniques inspired by the Mediterranean and Black Sea regions merged in the 3rd century BC in a taste for jewelry covered in pseudo-filigree and knobbly protrusions. Virtuosity in casting bronze reached an exceptionally high level, and the fully modeled style flourished.

New types of personal ornament appeared, such as women's belts made with heavy, finely worked links and enameled pendants. Cast bracelets and ankle rings with hollow clasps and oval bosses were all the rage in the Danube area in Bohemia and Germany. These inspired rings decorated with baroque reliefs and spirals, sometimes arranged in triangles from which human faces projected.

At the same time Celtic warriors were confronting the Greek art world, Hungary was the source of a new type of art found on sword scabbards. This spread west to Switzerland, across Gaul and into Britain, and eastward into the Balkans. The basic new theme was two imaginary animals—dragons, bipeds with an erect tail or penis, or spindly birds—positioned face to face. These magical motifs

A late-3rd-century BC bronze fibula from Slovenia (left) is treated in pseudo-filigree. This was an effect obtained by casting rather than individually positioning very fine threads. This style of decoration was adopted by the western Celts and appears again on some jewelry in Champagne.

The dome of this helmet (opposite) from Agris displays palmette designs incorporating coral studs fixed in place with silver rivets. Coral inlays also decorate the cheek pieces on which beaded threads form flowers and ram-headed snakes.

were sometimes inlaid or plated with gold and shifted subtly between plant and animal shapes.

The shoe was a much-prized Celtic symbol. Shown here in the form of a 3rd-century BC Hungarian vase, it also crops up on fibulae, especially at Hallein, in Austria.

On to New Pastures

The Macedonian empire, based in northern Greece, stood in the way of Celtic expansion for a long time. In the 4th century BC the Celts kept to northwestern Hungary, southwestern Slovakia, and part of Transylvania. But when Alexander the Great died in 323 BC, they moved on. The conflicts that riddled the Hellenic world after his death offered employment for mercenaries, all the more welcome to the Celts because the situation in Italy was beginning to turn sour. Transalpine Celts in search of adventure turned to the Atlantic, but even more to the Balkans.

At the beginning of the 3rd century BC an initial invasion of Thrace, to the northeast of Macedonia, ended in failure. The major onslaught then came in 280 BC when three separate groups attacked in concert. Thrace and the lands of the Triballi were invaded by Celts under their leader Cerethrius; Illyria and Macedonia by Bolgios' warriors; and Paeonia by troops under Brennus and Acichorius. Probably entering Macedonia along the Morava Valley, the Celts inflicted a bitter defeat upon Ptolemy Ceraunus's army; he himself was captured and beheaded.

In the famous legend the god Apollo appeared with a crash at the crucial moment when the Celts were about to plunder his temple's treasure. The Celts undoubtedly coveted Delphi's gold. The same event as seen by a Gallo-Roman potter (below) and by a 19th-century painter (opposite).

The Gold of Delphi

After this victory the Celtic army split in two. Brennus took advantage of the opening and swept into Greece, but his southward march was interrupted by battles, and he suffered heavy losses of men. After passing through Thermopylae with his troops, he launched a raid on Delphi in 279 BC, the notoriety of which reached epic proportions. It was a disaster. One legend relates that Apollo

himself wrought a miracle to avert sacrilege; another says that Delphi was sacked and its treasures carried off into Gaul. Brennus was killed. Another detachment of Celts that stayed in Thrace was defeated in 277 BC and turned back into Bulgaria, where they founded the short-lived kingdom of Tylis.

Thus ended the great Celtic invasion of Greece. Groups of armed men drifted around, some finding employment as mercenaries. Other minor

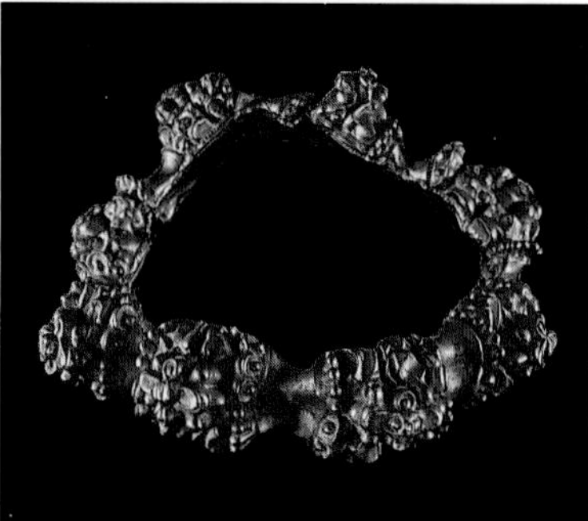

campaigns have not left many archaeological traces, but enough to confirm the identity of invaders from the Danube area.

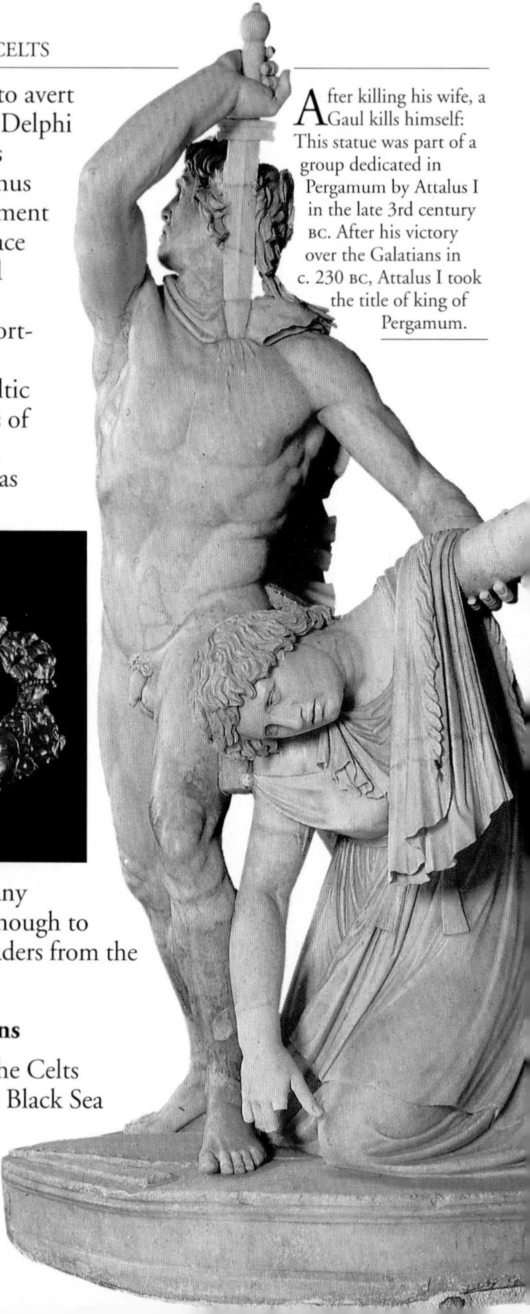

Eastern Celts and Galatians

The relationship between the Celts and the peoples around the Black Sea was more peaceful. There may have been trading contact, especially along the Danube. Certain shared cultural features—

After killing his wife, a Gaul kills himself: This statue was part of a group dedicated in Pergamum by Attalus I in the late 3rd century BC. After his victory over the Galatians in c. 230 BC, Attalus I took the title of king of Pergamum.

like the custom of head-hunting—or appreciable influences in the decoration of luxury items prove that ideas were exchanged and goods circulated.

The Galatians, a group of Celts who crossed into Asia Minor, did try to fit into the Hellenic world. Some troops of Brennus's army joined up with Nicomedes I (reigned 278–50 BC) of Bithynia, who settled them in an area between his own kingdom and that of Antiochus I (reigned 280–61 BC) of Syria. This settlement brought only trouble and provoked constant hostilities. The Galatians were driven back toward the high plateaus—the poorest area of Asia Minor—where they terrorized the larger towns. They meddled in the affairs of the local Hellenic states around 240 BC and even attacked Pergamum, but were defeated several times. Strongly Hellenized and far from their original homes, the Galatians eventually formed an isolated enclave that is said by ancient writers to have preserved its Celtic language and traditions well into the Christian era.

A recent study connected with the restoration of *The Dying Gaul* (below), a late 3rd-century BC statue, has questioned the traditional view that it is a marble copy of a bronze original made for the sanctuary at Pergamum. In fact the marble, which comes from Asia Minor, and the statue's superb artistry suggest that this is the original work after all.

Opposite left: The fine gold of this bracelet from Lasgraïsses, in southern France, is said to have come from the treasure of Delphi. It is a sample of Celtic goldworking dating from the 3rd and 2nd centuries BC. Jewelry in this florid sculptural style has been found very occasionally in the former Yugoslavia.

Crossing the Pyrenees

Archaeological evidence in southwestern France reveals Celtic infiltration from the East as early as the 5th century BC—chariot burials as far as the confines of Poitou and a scattering of typically

Found in the Tarn River, in southern France, this late-3rd-century BC bracelet (left) bears an unmistakable likeness to those made by the eastern Celts, from whom it may perhaps have been imported.

Celtic fibulae into the heart of the Pyrenees. This influence was sporadic until the 3rd century BC, when a new culture emerged. The ancient settlements of Toulouse and Agen were Celtic strongholds, and gold torques found in southern France confirm their arrival there.

That Celts crossed the Pyrenees and settled in the Iberian Peninsula (Spain and Portugal) is proved by a combination of ancient texts, linguistics, and place-names. Iberian Celts occupied the central regions of the peninsula, but other areas were also affected: In Portugal there are still traces of an archaic Celtic dialect. The Celts seem to have arrived in the region known as Galicia, in northwestern Spain, in the mid-1st century BC. This area was thus Celticized relatively late, but defended sites and hoards of torques from as early as 500 BC have been found. Perhaps these are signs of the reaction to the arrival of the first Celtic settlers. Massive "Celtiberic" sculptures have come from these strongholds. They portray wild boars, bulls, and highly stylized warriors holding shields and wearing torques.

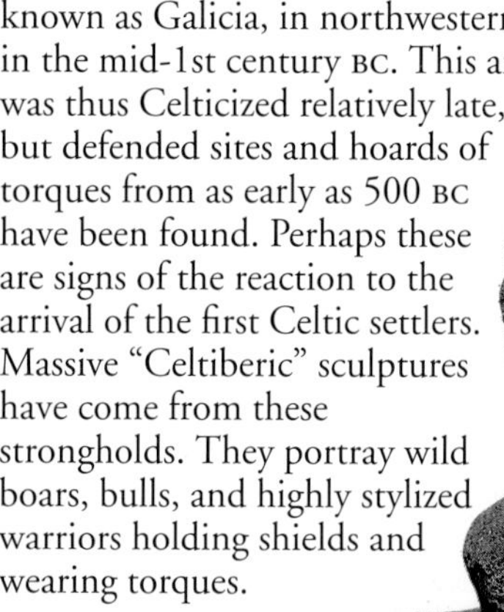

A Celtic warrior? This stone statue (below) from Castro do Lezenho, in Portugal, dating from the 2nd or 1st century BC, portrays a man whose torque and shield resemble those of Celtic statuary.

Armorica

Throughout the Bronze Age the Atlantic regions of Europe shared a culture and an

economy. These areas are rich in natural resources, especially tin, whose fame had reached the Mediterranean world and attracted many explorers. Armorica—on the French coast between the Seine and the Loire rivers—entered the Celtic sphere between the 5th and 4th centuries BC. Fragments of wine flagons and weapons found in the cemetery at Tronoën and gold beads from an underground chamber at Tréglonou suggest regular contact with Celts further inland, although strong regional distinctions still remained. Armorican Breton, the only Celtic language still spoken in continental Europe, is the best surviving evidence that the area did belong to what was once a vast Celtic province. The very fine local pottery long continued to be inspired by metal wares from northern Italy.

In the 4th century BC Armorican pottery was strongly influenced by Italo-Celtic bronze vessels with stamped decoration. Curvilinear decoration on this vase (above left) from a grave at Kervenez, on the French coast, suggests inspiration by the vegetal style.

A 5th-century BC bronze dagger sheath (above right) from Kernavest, another Celtic site on France's coastline.

The Roman military eagle spread its wings across the Alps. Soon Caesar was threatening Gaul. Consternation spread among the Celtic tribes, who gathered together behind one man—Vercingetorix. His defeat at Alesia in 52 BC signaled the demise of Celtic Europe, and the vanquished tribes crossed the water to lay down the remnants of their ancient culture in Britain and Ireland.

CHAPTER IV

THE CELTS AGAINST THE MIGHT OF ROME

The Romans, disciplined in fighting methods, went into battle (opposite) wearing breastplates with metal parts. Bare-chested and reckless, the Celts met them protected only by helmets and shields.

To enhance their power and magical charm, some of the swords and daggers were given anthropomorphic hilts, with human heads between brackets that suggest stylized arms and legs (right).

Early in the 2nd century BC the Roman conquest and assimilation of Cisalpine Gaul was completed. After seventy years of resistance the Iberian Peninsula also submitted, in 133 BC. The task of connecting Italy with the new Spanish provinces by land could begin.

The Conquest of Narbonensis

On the south coast of Gaul, Rome had a loyal ally in Massilia (the Latin form of the Greeks' Massalia, now Marseilles), a city that was having difficulty both in protecting its sea trade from attacks by Ligurian pirates and in defending itself on land from the troublesome Gauls. Massilia made a first appeal to Rome for help in 154 BC, and the Ligurian tribes that were besieging its colonies around Nice and Antibes were repulsed. When the conflict was settled, Rome withdrew. A generation later, in 125 BC, Massilia made a new appeal for help against the Celto-Ligurian Salluvii, who were defeated in 124 when the Romans took their stronghold at Entremont. The most powerful Gallic people on the west bank of the Rhone, the Allobroges, gave refuge to the Salluvii. In 122 a fresh Roman army went up against both tribes, and, despite the intervention of Bituitus, king of the Celtic Arverni, crossed the Alps and was victorious.

The hegemony that the Arverni tribe claimed to hold over Gaul forced the Romans to move in.

In Narbonensis, an area conquered by Rome in 121 BC, towns soon bore a Greco-Roman stamp. Neighboring peoples, except for the Ligurians in the south, were Celtic—the Volcae in the west and the Allobroges in the northeast. Above left is a present-day view of Glanum, a small town with lively trade that was destroyed by the Romans in 125 BC and then was rebuilt and became active during the Gallo-Roman period.

Bituitus gathered 300,000 men to meet them, but the battle ended in disaster for the Gauls. Rome was able to set up the province of Gallia Narbonensis, or Provincia (now Provence), on annexed territory along the Mediterranean coast between Italy and the Pyrenees; the port of Narbo (modern-day Narbonne) became its capital.

Having beaten the Romans at Noricum, the fearsome Germanic Cimbri were finally defeated at Vercelli, in Piedmont (engraving left), where they were crushed by Roman general Marius's army in 101 BC.

The conquest of Narbonensis facilitated Roman trade between Massilia and the south. Between 75 and 60 BC a 130-foot-long ship sank near Hyères, in southeastern France, with its cargo (below and left). It is the largest ancient wreck found off the French coast. Excavation started in 1972, and the ship proved to contain 6000 amphorae of Italian wine as well as crates of pottery vessels.

A Twofold Danger: Germania and Rome

In the east, another threat was looming—the invasions of the Germanic Cimbri and Teuton tribes, which lasted from 113 to 101 BC. The Cimbri came from the shores of the North Sea and Jutland, while the Teutons, originally from the Baltic coastline, had perhaps already settled permanently around the Main River, in northern

Bavaria. The Cimbri were driven back from Bavaria and Bohemia by the Celtic tribe of the Boii. They reached the Celtic state of Noricum to the east of the Alps and then headed for Italy. The Romans were finally able to halt their advance in 101 BC, but Gaul emerged from the ordeal worn out and in disarray.

The Suevi, another Germanic people, reached Alsace, in northeastern France, in around 70 BC. Around 61 or 60 BC their ferocious king, Ariovistus, inflicted a severe defeat upon a Gallic army. Another enemy arose in southeastern Europe: The Dacians (ancestors of the Romanians), under their king Burebista, overwhelmed the Celtic populations of the Danube basin. Around 60 BC the Dacians in Austria made an alliance with Ariovistus, who had already united other tribes from central and northern Germany. Faced with imminent danger,

the Celtic Aedui appealed for Roman support; other Celtic peoples reacted differently.

The Dramatic Migration of the Helvetii

Under this mounting threat, the Helvetii of western Switzerland, described by Greek historian Posidonius in the 1st century BC as "rich in gold but a peaceful people," decided in 58 BC to leave Switzerland for southwestern France, in one of the last great Celtic migrations. Originally from the east, probably from the Black Forest, they had started moving fifty years earlier to flee the Germanic advance.

Thousands now left their villages, setting them afire, and assembled at the tip of the Lake of Geneva. Many other neighboring Celtic peoples joined them near Genava (now Geneva), a strategically placed Allobrogan stronghold. Their numbers rose to 368,000, of whom 92,000 were fighting men. They planned to cross the Rhone by the Genava bridge and

Called in to help the Aedui, Caesar drove the Suevi from Alsace in 58 BC. Opposite above: Caesar meets Ariovistus, king of the Germanic Suevi.

A large oak figure (opposite below), dated c. 80 BC, supposedly a protective deity, was retrieved from the port of Geneva. Discovery of another similar statue has suggested the function of enormous torques like this one found in Basel (below left). Hollow and with large terminals, these objects once had an iron core coated in resin and clay, thus limiting the amount of gold needed while giving an impression of solid mass.

The Helvetii burned the ramparts of Mont Vully (below) with torches in 58 BC before leaving for Genava.

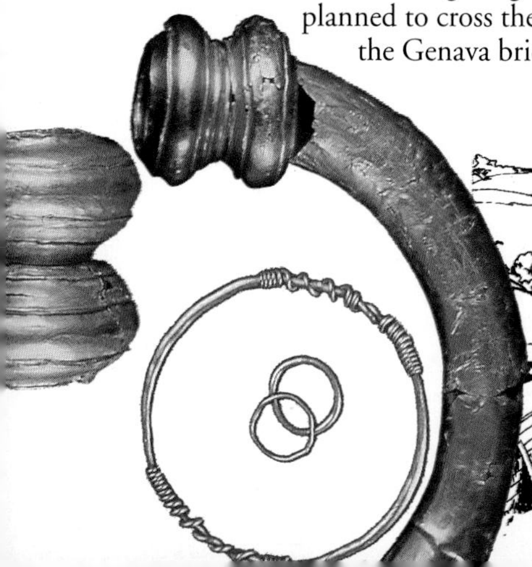

follow the river south into friendly territory.

Julius Caesar (102–44 BC), governor of the Roman province, heard of their project, went to Genava, and cut the bridge. Attempts at negotiation failed. The Helvetii then tried to move north with their 2800 ox carts but were attacked and massacred by the Roman legions. Divico, their chief, asked for a truce. Caesar demanded hostages. Divico replied that the Helvetii were accustomed to taking, not giving, hostages, and war was renewed. A rumor started that the Roman legions were retreating. But the Helvetian offensive became a rout, and in the end they surrendered. Caesar ordered the survivors to go back to their abandoned lands and rebuild their houses.

In 55 BC Caesar built a bridge over the Rhine to enable him to push through to the east.

Gaul was not homogeneous at the time of the conquest: There were the Belgae in the north, the Armoricans in the west, and the so-called Gauls in the center. In the south was the Narbonensis region, only part of which was Celtic. The southwest was essentially Aquitanian, despite several Celtic enclaves around Bordeaux and Agen. The Parisii tribe occupied an area between the Belgae, the Armoricans, and the Gauls.

The Struggle for Independence

Once called in for help against the Germanic tribes, Caesar never looked back. He had gained a foothold in Gaul and needed to secure his political position in Rome. Without provocation he mounted a campaign against the Belgae, the most powerful people in Gaul: Some, alarmed by the unexpected attack, surrendered. Others assembled an army but were defeated on the Aisne River, in northern France, and pushed back.

At the same time, Caesar, who had come under

Portus Itius
MENAPII
NERVII
EBURONES
ADUATUCI
MORINI
Nemetocenna
(Arras)
ATREBATES
BELGIUM
TREVERI
AMBIANI
Samarobriva
(Amiens)
CALETES
VELIOCASSES
Bratuspantium
BELLOVACI
REMI
MEDIOMATRICI
LEXOVII
Noviodunum
(Soissons)
Durocortorum
(Reims)
AULERCI
EBUROVICES
PARISII
SUESSIONES
Lutetia
(Paris)
Metlosedum
(Melun)
AULERCI
DIABLINTES
LEUCI
CARNUTES
SENONES
Agedincum
(Sens)
Vellaunodunum
AULERCI
CENOMANI
LINGONES
Cenabum
(Orléans)
MANDUBII
Noviodunum
Alesia
ANDES
Vesontio
(Besançon)
BITURIGES
AEDUI
Gorgobina
TURONES
Avaricum
(Bourges)
Noviodunum
Bibracte
SEQUANI
HELVETII
Decetia
Cabillonum
(Châlon-sur-Saône)
Matisco
(Mâcon)
AMBARRI
Genava
(Geneva)
CELTIC GAUL
Gergovia
SEGUSIAVI
LEMOVICES
Vienna
ARVERNI
ALLOBROGES
PETROCORII
Uxellodunum?
(Issoudun)
TRANSALPINE GAUL
CADURCI
RUTENI
AUSCI
Tolosa
(Toulouse)
Massalia
(Marseilles)
Narbo
(Narbonne)

heavy attack by the Nervii in the north, also sent legions to Armorica to subjugate the maritime peoples, decimate their fleet, and isolate central Gaul. When Caesar returned unsuccessful from Britain at the end of 54 BC, he found a worsening situation in Gaul: Unrest was stirring among the Carnutes, the Senones, and the Eburones further north. He tried to take control and, so as not to lose face, announced to Rome that order reigned in Gaul. But, even at such a distance, his vain claims were doubted, and satirical pamphlets were circulated by his detractors.

Vercingetorix, the Gauls' Last Hope

Informed by Caesar's critics of Roman attitudes toward him, the Gauls conspired. The Carnutes proposed a general rebellion. Druids, the ancient Celtic priests, gathered in forests and predicted success in a sacred war for independence. A leader was chosen: Vercingetorix, an Arvernian prince, son of Celtillus, who had been put to death by his compatriots for attempting to reinstate the kingship. Still in his youth, Vercingetorix had been with Caesar's army among the Gallic contingents sent by

A gold coin of 52 BC inscribed with Vercingetorix's name (below) shows an idealized portrait of the young chief. Twenty-seven of these coins are known to exist.

Like many 19th-century painted or sculpted portraits of warriors, this painting, *Vercingetorix Summons the Gauls to the Defense of Alesia* (detail, left), by François Ehrmann, is inspired not by equipment of the period but by anachronistic objects at least half a millennium older, probably because of the more advanced state of Early Iron Age excavations at the time the painting was being made. The arm ring, the belt of stamped sheet bronze, and the sword all date from around 600 BC; the helmet, older still, is a type from the Italian Late Bronze Age. The torque is the only Late Iron Age accessory.

various peoples as proof of their allegiance.

As soon as he was elected leader of the Gallic resistance, Vercingetorix agitated for winning over the majority of central Gaul and Armorica and organizing all of Gaul for the great uprising. He had detailed plans that including cutting the Roman army's lines of communication between Italy and Gaul by launching a simultaneous offensive against Narbonensis, the Aedui, and Caesar's legions. But Caesar's speed thwarted these plans. Provincia had had time to prepare its defense, and Vercingetorix was forced to turn back.

This silver coin (both sides shown at left) of c. 50 BC, minted by the Aedui, is in the name of their chief, Dubnorex (Dumnorix). The reverse shows a triumphant figure holding the head of a vanquished enemy in one hand and a carnyx (a sort of war horn) and wild-boar emblem in the other. Dubnorex, initially Caesar's ally, finally rallied to the cause of his compatriots.

The Bituriges were unwilling to sacrifice their stronghold at Avaricum (present-day Bourges) by implementing the scorched-earth policy advocated by Vercingetorix. Thus, despite a heroic stand, the town was taken, and 40,000 of its inhabitants perished. This disaster taught the Gauls a lesson, and Vercingetorix's authority was reinforced.

The Romans set up effective blockades before Avaricum (left), capital of the Bituriges, which finally fell in 52 BC.

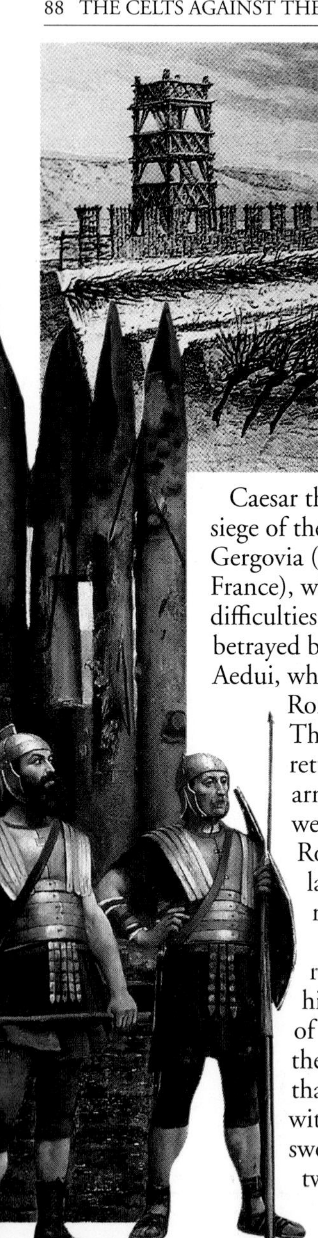

Caesar then embarked upon the siege of the chief Arvernian citadel, Gergovia (in southern central France), which presented great difficulties. What is more, he was betrayed by his former allies the Aedui, who massacred all the Romans in their territory. Thwarted, he decided to return to Provincia with his armies. Just when the Gauls were about to chase the Romans from their lands, a reckless escapade reversed their fortunes.

Vercingetorix, who had remained in the rear with his infantry, let loose three of his cavalry corps to harass the Romans and make sure that they departed. Heady with victory, the cavalry swore not to return without twice passing through the enemy column.

This sketch of Alesia (above) was made by order of French emperor Napoleon III (1808–73). Here, on the border between the Lingones and the Aedui, Vercingetorix took refuge in 52 BC. The Roman army besieged it, encircling the town with two lines of defense reinforced by ditches and a third outside line directed against the relief army. Between the two ditches a whole network of spikes was arranged, while holes dug in the earth allowed the movements of the Gauls to be closely monitored.

They had forgotten that Germanic auxiliaries had come to Caesar's aid and that the Roman army never let itself be taken by surprise. The Roman troops turned around and pursued the Gallic cavalry back to Vercingetorix's camp. Shattered, the Gauls took refuge in Alesia, citadel of the Mandubii.

Gaul's Last Hours of Liberty

Vercingetorix sent his cavalry back with the task of enlisting men from every tribe and state for a final contest. He shut himself in Alesia with 80,000 high-ranking warriors and enough supplies for thirty days, awaiting reinforcements from all of Gaul. Meanwhile, around the citadel the Romans constructed a network of lines of defense that neither the besieged warriors nor the reinforcements were able to cross.

Vercingetorix's orders were not well understood, and the general levy was too late. When at last help arrived, the besieged men were at the end of their strength. Several battles took place, but without any real strategic coordination. The Gallic forces were routed, and the various contingents fled, each returning to its own community. For Vercingetorix this meant abandonment, defeat, and despair.

During the following months Caesar was absorbed in using force to quell the lingering resistance of the Bituriges, Carnutes, and the Bellovaci. In Poitou, Limousin, and Cahors he also met desperate last stands. But Gaul had finally fallen. So Celtic Europe suffered unstable conditions, and its territory was greatly reduced during the 1st century BC.

According to Caesar, Vercingetorix's surrender took place between guards at the gates of the Roman camp (below and opposite). Mounted on his horse, Vercingetorix galloped across the space between the two camps. He rode a circle to the right around the tribunal, as though magically to bind his conqueror, then cast his arms without a word at the startled proconsul's feet. Though Caesar gave only a dry account of Vercingetorix's surrender, the nobility of his deed was raised to legendary status by historians from Livy to Plutarch, especially as he enabled many of his companions to flee (above left) by distracting the Romans.

First having copied Macedonian coins, Celtic coin makers soon gave free rein to their creativity. The front sides of these coins show heads sprouting shocks of curly hair. On the reverse the conventional horse team often gave way to fantasy, such as a horse with a giant bird or a human-headed horse. The first issues were fairly heavy coins of pure metal. Some Celtic tribes, such as the Parisii, used gold. Others used triple alloys of copper, gold, and silver, or even, like the Cenomani, kept the appearance of gold by plating over a base alloy. Outside their own area, coins were worth only the weight of the metal they contained, a fact that explains why sensitive scales are often found at settlements.

After taking Gaul, the Romans occupied Pannonia in 12 BC. Then, in Bohemia and Moravia, the Germani wiped out a Celtic civilization already radically altered by the Dacians.

The British Isles

There is evidence in Britain of the first arrival of Celts in the 5th century BC. Equipment very similar to that found in Champagne from the same period has been discovered there: daggers with decorated sheaths and fibulae made by artisans from the Marne River region. It seems likely that it was groups from Belgic Gaul that Celticized the British Isles. Indeed, two Celtic groups in Britain bear the names of continental Belgic tribes: the Parisii (from around Paris) in Yorkshire and the Atrebates (from around Arras) south of the Thames in Hampshire and Sussex. Commius, king of the Atrebates, who once had assisted Caesar, later became one of the leaders of the anti-Roman Gallic coalition and eventually took refuge in Britain.

Boudicea, queen of the Iceni of East Anglia, killed herself in AD 61 after a failed rebellion against the Romans.

These Celtic populations in Britain successfully opposed Caesar's ambitions with their armies of chariots. Emperor Claudius I's legions embarked upon an ultimately successful conquest in AD 43, but British resistance continued for some time. In AD 61 a rebellion led by Boudicea, queen of the Iceni tribe of East Anglia, attacked the towns of Camulodunum (now Colchester) and Londinium (London) and massacred entire Roman garrisons, but it, too, was finally suppressed. By AD 77 Britain—except for the Welsh mountains and northern Scotland—had been brought under Roman rule; Ireland was untouched and would remain profoundly Celtic.

Irish literature bears witness to its Celtic legacy. After writing was introduced to them—allegedly by Christian missionary St. Patrick in 432—Irish poets committed the ancient oral tradition to the written—manuscript—page.

The numerous forts on the Irish coastline may date from the Celtic Iron Age. Opposite above: The stone ramparts of Oghil, in Ireland, date from between the 1st and 5th centuries AD.

This early 1st-century AD horned bronze helmet (left), found near Waterloo Bridge in London, was put in the river as a votive offering. A very rare specimen, its striking appearance has led to its being widely used in popular images of the Gauls. Some headdresses from Ireland with two or three bronze horns may be sacred crowns.

From Brittany to Britain

Found in the Thames, the Battersea shield was never used for combat. Its symmetrical design, glass inlay, and interlacing are peculiar to British Celtic art of the 1st century AD.

Some carved granite standing stones in continental Europe allow links to be made with Celtic art in the British Isles: The decorated geometric panels on a 4th-century BC stone found in Trégastel or on the Kermaria stone at Pont-l'Abbé, both on the French coast, seem to derive from the same source of inspiration as five standing stones in Ireland dated between the 3rd and 1st centuries BC.

There is little evidence for Celtic art in the British Isles before the 4th or even 3rd centuries BC, and it was only in the 2nd century BC that British art attained a sophisticated style, traces of which are found on weapons such as sword scabbards and large shields. In the 1st century BC two currents became clear, one characterized by stylized human or animal elements and the other by a whole series of abstract shapes and patterns governed by the use of compasses. Art on the backs of mirrors illustrates the climax of this refined technique. While on the Continent the conventions of Greco-Roman art gradually imposed a leaning toward sobriety, a so-called severe style, the Celtic tradition remained firmly rooted in Britain for a long time, even after its partial conquest.

In Ireland, remote from Roman influence, Celtic culture stayed intact, and Late Iron Age art merged imperceptibly with Christian art. Small bronze

Bronze mirrors with sumptuously worked backs were a specialty of workshops in southern England between the 1st century BC and the 1st century AD. Above the openwork handle spreads a sophisticated pattern that frames plain smooth areas with grooved basketwork motifs.

objects—boxes, pins, or bridle bits—perpetuated Celtic decorative motifs. There are bronze disks whose use is still a mystery. Irish jewelry in the early Middle Ages, especially circular brooches and trimmings, still bore designs of Iron Age inspiration: heads of water birds, curvilinear patterns, and S shapes. This

Enigmatic carved stones may be relics of ancient sacred beliefs about the universe. Irish stones are usually three or four centuries more recent than Armorican examples. A squat pyramid from Kermaria of the 4th century BC (near left) has a different design on each of its four faces. The rounded Turoe stone (far left) from the 1st century BC in Galway, Ireland, has vegetal motifs exactly like much older continental jewelry.

Celtic taste for decorative virtuosity was to continue in the art of manuscript illumination.

The Oppida: Fortified Towns

The first Celtic towns, protected by ramparts, developed almost everywhere in Gaul. Urban life took shape in the specialized quarters laid out along the streets: artisans' houses, buildings of various sorts with religious functions, and assembly places. A sort of bourgeoisie that produced and consumed semi-luxury goods and held political power emerged. A central oppidum served as the capital of a region, and it was there that coinage was made and exchanged. The proliferation of coin types reveals the subdivision of territories and the increasing autonomy of small political units.

The network of land and river communications spread quickly. Mass-produced craft goods (such as fibulae) and imported Mediterranean products (such as wine and oil) came into general use and betray the growing influence of the Roman world nearby.

Part of the population must have lived on the proceeds of trade, but it is not known whether artisans were free and independent or attached to the noble, or equestrian, class. One of the functions of these fortified towns was to protect strategic points in this fragile economy by serving as stopping-places, centers of attraction on the main communication

The artisans' quarters and marketplaces were on the outskirts of oppida. At Bibracte, a site in eastern France, an enameler's workshop was found next to a bronzesmith's. There were melting pots, coloring matter, iron tongs, and scraps of glass. Bibracte is the only oppidum to have yielded so much evidence of glasswork.

Rings colored violet (manganese), green (copper), blue (cobalt), and yellow (lead) prove that Celtic glassworkers knew how to handle oxides (opposite center).

The Aeduan capital, Bibracte (left), was an important oppidum, 27 acres in size. Vercingetorix was given command there by the assembly of Gallic chiefs, and it was there, after the battle of Alesia, that Caesar took up winter quarters and began to write his *Commentaries on the Gallic War.*

routes, and refuges for the local population. But who governed the oppida—kings, princes, or an aristocracy? It seems that the situation differed from one region to another, although in general power seems to have fallen into the hands of merchant nobles.

An Abundance of Natural Wealth

In the countryside quarries began to be exploited—for clay

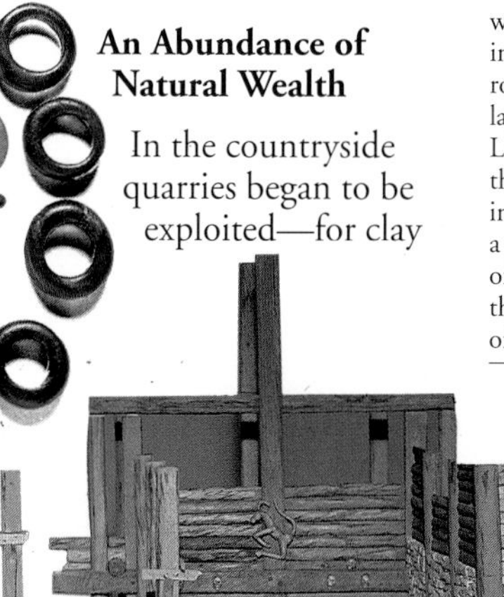

The *murus gallicus* (reconstruction below), which was built to fortify a tribe's capital, is a peculiarly Celtic type of rampart. It has a wooden framework of intersecting beams whose rows are separated by layers of earth or rubble. Long iron nails pinned the beams at each intersection. It was given a cladding of large blocks of close-fitting stone through which the ends of the beams protruded.

The blacksmith held a privileged position among craftspeople. Huge numbers of iron tools and weapons were made from the 2nd century BC onward: axes, swords, spearheads, parts of shields, the chains that attached sword scabbards to the belt, and jewelry, including plenty of brooches. The power of the aristocracy was based on its possession of iron, used not only for the production of arms and armor but also for all the agricultural equipment that was needed to till the land. On the far left, on an iron sword blade of c. 100 BC, is an oval stamp with a pair of goats confronting each other, probably the blacksmith's trademark. His name, Korisios, is also inscribed in Greek letters. This is one of the oldest examples of writing north of the Alps.

to make pottery, marl to spread on fields, and stone for building or sculpture. Even if the intensive use of naturally abundant woodland led to excessive deforestation, the Gauls were discriminating in the use they made of wood. They were responsible for inventing the barrel and excelled in the manufacturing of chariots.

The indigenous farm was the essential setting for all kinds of agricultural activities, which developed and flourished in a green and hospitable countryside scattered with woods and sources of water. Hunting provided for only a small part

The Gallic site of Villeneuve-St.-Germain (left) was an oppidum lying just above water level, almost surrounded by the Aisne River and barred to the south by a rampart. Intensively occupied after the Roman conquest, from 50 to 15 BC, it is typical of built-up settlements, with long thatched buildings separated by occasional gaps. Recent excavations have revealed where coins were made and where bronzesmiths, blacksmiths, carpenters, and furriers worked. The remains of glass beads and little wheels have also been uncovered.

Iron knives and sheepshears from La Tène dating from the 3rd or 2nd century BC.

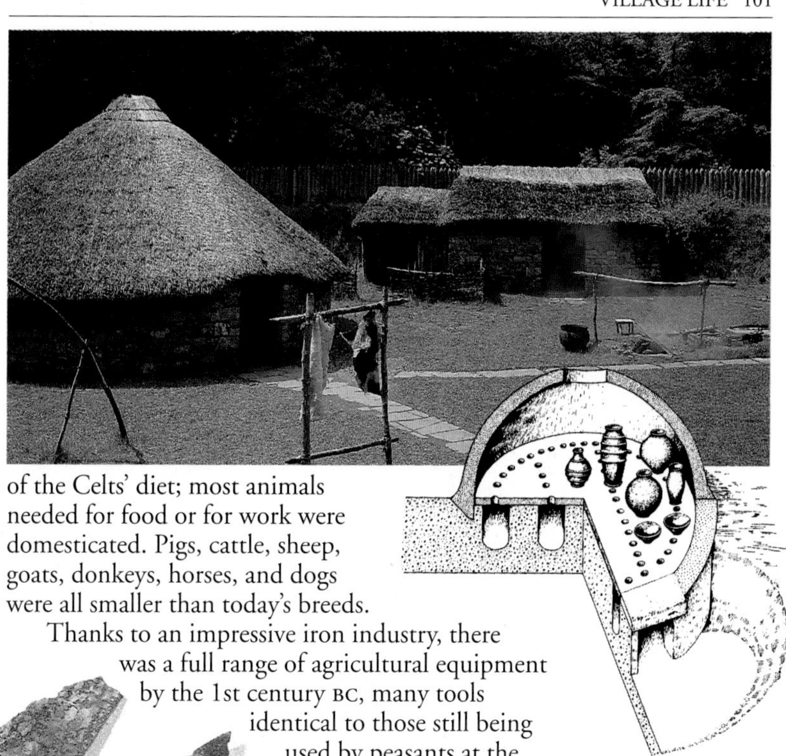

of the Celts' diet; most animals needed for food or for work were domesticated. Pigs, cattle, sheep, goats, donkeys, horses, and dogs were all smaller than today's breeds.

Thanks to an impressive iron industry, there was a full range of agricultural equipment by the 1st century BC, many tools identical to those still being used by peasants at the beginning of the 20th century. In some areas fields were fertilized and enriched. In addition to the swing plough, there was a wheeled plough to improve yields. The scythe and sickle were sometimes replaced by an animal-drawn reaping machine called a *vallus*. Villages multiplied, especially on the plains, with thatched wooden houses, grain-storage pits, and enclosed animal pasture. Some isolated and defended farms were also aristocratic households.

In experimental farms such as the one near Quin, in Ireland (top), Celtic farming, stock-raising, building, and craft techniques are studied.

To improve firing, kilns with two separate chambers (drawing above) had a combustion chamber below and a space above where unfired pots could be placed.

There are terrifying ancient accounts of Celtic groves inhabited by the gods. There the wind never blew on the trees, birds were frightened to perch on the branches, and the world was filled with icy shadows that the sun never pierced. Monuments and religious practices reveal the complexity of the Celtic mind. Despite the cruel demands of their gods, the Celts remained confident of the soul's immortality.

CHAPTER V
REALMS OF RELIGION

A sheet-bronze statue, about 28 inches high, of a warrior god (right) was recently found in a sanctuary at St.-Maur-en-Chaussée, a Celtic site in northern France. The metal contains a lot of zinc, like some coins of the 1st century AD. Hexagonal pieces similar to the statue's shield were also found deposited as offerings. The figure's symmetrical hairstyle in thick strands resembles the hair on stone statues from southern France —such as these 2nd-century BC severed heads (opposite) from the Entremont sanctuary—where the styles of classical Italy and the Celto-Ligurians merged.

Celtic sanctuaries were sacred spaces cut off from the rest of the world. Sometimes simple natural places like a mountain, lake, or clearing, they can also be identified by architectural features, though little usually survives apart from the faint marks of postholes where wooden structures once stood. Archaeologists have distinguished four types of sanctuary: *Viereckschanzen,* or quadrangular enclosures; sanctuaries of the Belgic or Picardy type, best known in northern France; the Celto-Ligurian sanctuaries of southern France; and sacred springs.

Ritual pits were dug by the Celts from the 4th century BC onward in sanctuaries like the *Viereckschanzen.* The custom of consigning the remains of burials and various offerings—animal bones, pottery, and metal or wooden objects—to the depths of the earth continued into the Gallo-Roman period, as the funerary pits at Vieille-Toulouse or at Bernard-en-Vendée (drawings left and opposite), where more than twenty have been found since 1858, bear witness.

Mysterious *Viereckschanzen*

These places, with their square shape (as their German name indicates) and bounded by one or more ditches or a bank of earth, normally contain almost nothing, apart from scraps of pottery, and are found from central France to Bohemia and Moravia. They have been particularly well studied in southern Germany, where they seem to have been used from the 4th to the 1st centuries BC; every year

This wooden statue of a stag (left) was found at the bottom of a pit at Fellbach-Schmiden, in southern Germany, along with various other animals rearing up on their hind legs. They probably formed part of a symmetrical carving.

more of them are discovered, usually using aerial photography. The complex arrangements inside these enclosures seem to follow no general pattern. Only the smallest of them (around 200 feet wide) have structural remains in the central area, where ritual shafts have sometimes been dug.

Belgic Theaters for Macabre Ceremonies

Some of the so-called Belgic or Picardy enclosures, used between the 3rd and 1st centuries BC, have produced many ritual offerings. These sites measure 100 to 150 feet along each side and are surrounded by ditches and a bank topped by a fence. At the center a wooden temple opens to the east. These temples were originally decorated with paintings or sculptures, and their walls were laden with prestigious displays of warriors' weapons. Texts by Caesar and the historian Livy suggest that in some temples war trophies were hung up by victorious tribes and might have remained on the sanctuary walls for several decades until they fell down. They were then smashed and thrown into a central pit.

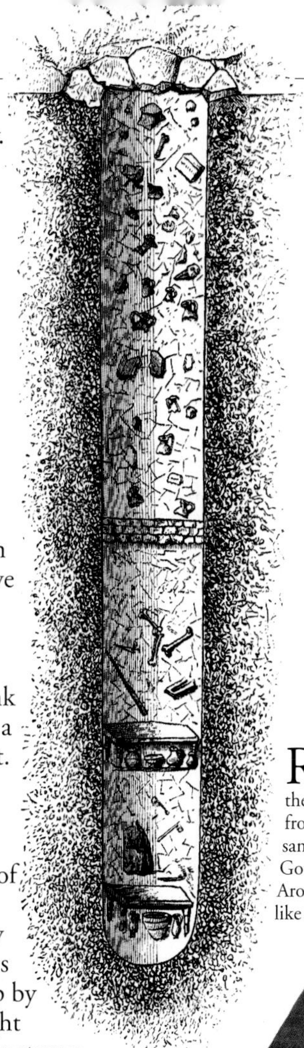

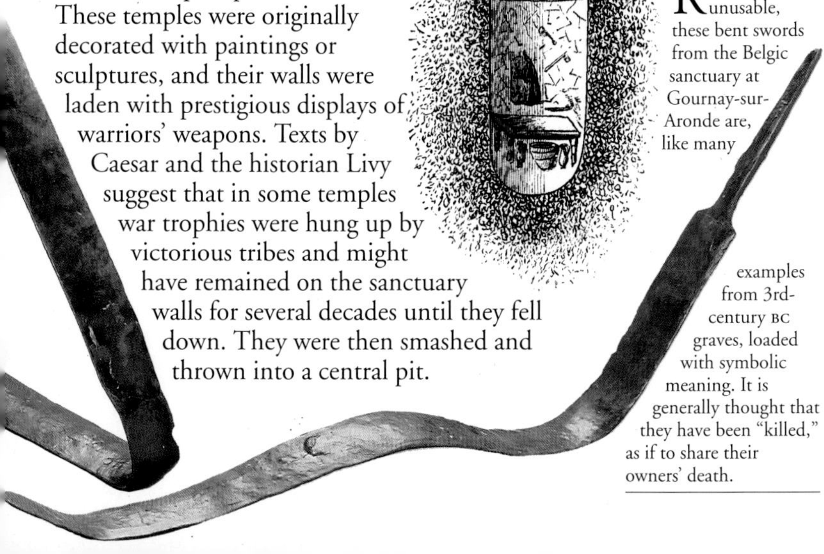

Rendered unusable, these bent swords from the Belgic sanctuary at Gournay-sur-Aronde are, like many examples from 3rd-century BC graves, loaded with symbolic meaning. It is generally thought that they have been "killed," as if to share their owners' death.

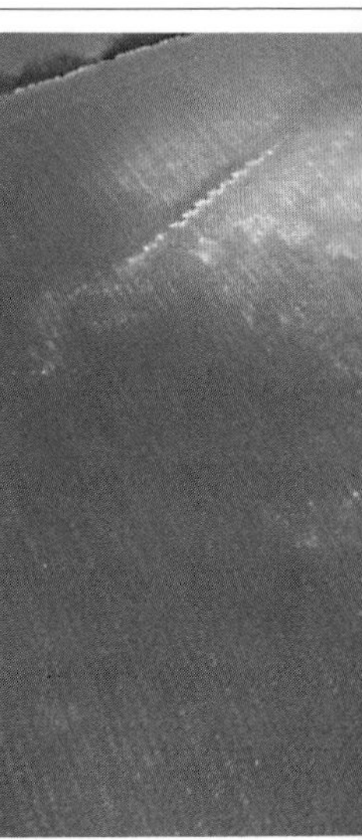

Domesticated horses first appeared in Gaul during the Bronze Age and were about the size of large ponies today. Caesar tells of the Gauls' great passion for horses and of how they even imported larger breeds. The high value accorded to horses was reflected in the Gauls' unusual ways of dealing with them when they died. They were neither eaten nor merely dumped, but carefully buried in pits.

At Gournay-sur-Aronde, the sanctuary inside the oppidum has yielded iron weapons and animal bones, the relics of numerous sacrifices scattered into its boundary ditches. Its entrance, carefully arranged at a gap in the ditch, consisted of a porch surmounted by trophies that included human skulls with their empty and terrifying stare.

Stacks of Bones

Animal sacrifices took different forms according to the animal, the season, and the divinity being honored. Oxen were the most common, especially old animals, but there were also plenty of bulls, killed by ax blows to the forehead. The whole carcass was put into the large pit in the temple and left until the bones detached. The skull was then displayed with warrior offerings and the rest of the skeleton was thrown into the ditch. Horses were also sacrificed. Sheep and pigs were reserved for consumption at the ritual feasts held on the site.

Human bones also performed ritual functions. One of the largest rural sanctuaries in Gaul was built in the 3rd century BC at Ribemont-sur-Ancre, in northern France. It was more than 2500 feet long, with a complex layout. Here long bones from about a

Very distinctive funerary rites and traces of sacrifice have come to light at a site in northern France (above, an aerial view of the sanctuary). An earthen bank marked the edge of an open ditch where headless and dismembered corpses of men and women must have been placed over a period of several decades at the end of the 3rd century BC. About a thousand young subjects with no apparent symptoms of disease were probably sacrificed. Their arm and leg bones, collected around a central post into which weapons and horses' bones were fitted, formed a strange cubic monument measuring over 5 feet each way.

thousand individuals aged fifteen to twenty years were stacked and crisscrossed into a sinister cubic monument, each side measuring over 5 feet. These community ossuaries made pillarlike structures at the four inside corners of the enclosure. Between each of these bone pillars dismembered bodies littered the ground; their skulls had been detached and treated. How these people died remains a mystery.

The Hero Cult

The 2nd-century BC Greek grammarian and poet Nicander noted that the Celts practiced divination (the art of foretelling events) at the tombs of their dead warriors, in which they would spend the night. In southern France a whole range of stone sculptures found in sanctuaries reveals the development of the ancient hero cult, already widespread in the 6th century BC, as the Hirschlanden stela (see p. 29) suggests.

Entremont, Roquepertuse, and Glanum, in Provence, are among the best known of these Celto-

Ligurian sanctuaries linked to oppida on the fringe of the Celtic world. Here, stone pillars with niches for human skulls, decorated lintels and painted sculptures of gods, warriors in breastplates or sitting cross-legged, and animals (birds or monsters) were originally part of an architectural complex. The sanctuary at Entremont was a long building shaped like a portico, with square columns that once

With half-closed eyes sunk in their sockets, long hair, and puckered mouth, the Entremont "severed head" (opposite) has an open hand resting upon it. This gesture might commemorate a victor taking possession of a vanquished enemy's remains. The most famous statue from the same sanctuary (center), nearly 30 inches tall, is of a squatting warrior wearing a breastplate. Left: Detail of a pillar carved with two stylized heads. Whether these monuments at Entremont were made before or after the Roman conquest remains undecided.

supported a roof. That at Roquepertuse, built on two terraces and in full use during the 3rd century BC, was burned down in the 2nd century BC, when Roman influence was increasing. Neither sacrificial remains nor typical ritual structures such as an altar or pit have been found. The presence of exposed human skulls is a point of similarity with the Belgic sanctuaries, but the statuary suggests that here they were dedicated to glorious heroes or ancestors.

Head-hunters?

The head occupied a special place in Celtic art and religion. A severed head with half-closed eyes, sometimes without a mouth,

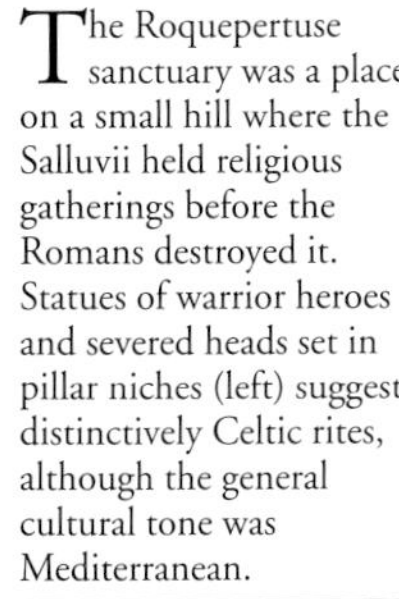

The Roquepertuse sanctuary was a place on a small hill where the Salluvii held religious gatherings before the Romans destroyed it. Statues of warrior heroes and severed heads set in pillar niches (left) suggest distinctively Celtic rites, although the general cultural tone was Mediterranean.

and carved in stone, is a common find at sanctuaries in southern France. Sometimes the hero grasped a head by the hair or rested a hand on it. Was he recalling his warrior exploits? Or is the head meant to symbolize his own death?

A valid explanation has yet to be found for the human skulls displayed at these sanctuaries. Were they select victims from within the tribe? Or the severed heads of enemies? There were accounts of how Celtic warriors would collect heads after battles: They would hang the heads of enemies they had killed across their horses' necks and later nail them up as trophies on the doors of their houses. They would preserve the heads of distinguished chiefs in cedar oil and show them off to strangers with pride.

In any event, the Celto-Ligurian sanctuaries clearly suggest that their demanding and pitiless religion had a bloodthirsty fascination with deified warrior heroes.

Divine Water

"Copious water falls from dark springs...and grim, shapeless images of gods are rough-hewn from tree trunks, rotten with age, whose eerie pallor is chilling." So said the Roman poet Lucan (AD 39–65), adding that none but the priest dared approach this grove near Marseilles, which was given over to the gods. Springs, ponds, caves, wells, and lakes were repositories of sacrificial gold and were actually privileged sacred places: The springs at Chamalières, in southern central France, and the headwaters of the Seine served as sanctuaries where hundreds of carved wooden votive offerings, jewelry, and coins were deposited, mostly after the Roman conquest.

The Gallo-Romans were in fact only continuing a cult that went back to the Bronze Age and was widely practiced by the Celts. The site at La Tène on the Lake of Neuchâtel was

probably one of these vast open-air sanctuaries that reappeared when the water level was low at the end of the 19th century. Near a small village two bridges that crossed the River Thielle in antiquity were the repositories of hundreds of iron weapons, especially swords; personal ornaments were rare by comparison.

Many human skeletons bear traces of wounds, which tends to rule out the suggestion that they died a natural death. Skulls of cattle and horses were specially selected in preference to long bones.

Jewelry Offerings

Precious goods collected as votive offerings, especially hoards of golden torques, reflect a ritual practiced across all of Celtic Europe, especially between the 4th and 1st centuries BC. The Erstfeld hoard in Switzerland, abandoned in an Alpine pass, typifies these sacrifices to nature: Here golden torques and bracelets decorated with mythological figures were

Wooden statues placed as votive offerings from the source of the Seine in the 1st century BC (center) were cloaked like pilgrims in a typically Gallic hooded cape or wore the traditional torque. Opposite below: A 1st-century BC miniature gold boat with movable mast and oars, from the Broighter treasure in Northern Ireland.

Among other bronzes from a site in northern France—including animals and a male figurine—a naked dancing girl skims the floor with all the grace of her 5 inches (left). This freedom of style dates the piece to the late 1st century BC, while the rest of the hoard seems to have been buried in the 3rd century AD.

consecrated to a mountain deity. In Bohemia the Duchcov hoard, found in a spring, like the Lauterach hoard from Austria, contained large quantities of women's jewelry, especially fibulae. Concentrations of hoards have come to light around Toulouse, in southwestern France, and in parts of southern and eastern England. Eight hoards were buried close to one another at Snettisham in Norfolk. One found in 1990 had about 70 pounds of precious metal, mostly base alloys of copper, gold, and silver.

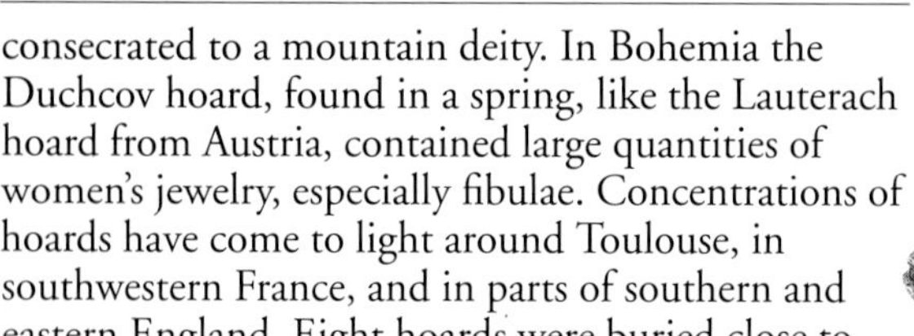

Coinage and Religion

The first Celtic gold coins from the 4th and especially the 3rd centuries BC were included in votive offerings and are often found associated with torques in France, Germany, and England. Scraps of mythology can be gleaned from coins. Some designs, full of meaning, contain surprising elements, especially on coins from Armorica: human heads with lines coming out of their foreheads, chains of dots ending in little floating heads, contorted figures, heads with monstrous eyes, or human-headed horses with imaginative harnesses.

A sacred shrub from the oppidum of Manching. This branch made of plated wood has side shoots bearing bronze ivy leaves thinly plated in gold. This cult object suggesting the sacred tree was carefully hidden in a wooden chest in the 3rd or 2nd century BC.

Some of the very earliest Celtic gold coins, issued in an area between southern Germany and Switzerland, were convex and decorated with magical designs (three globules or a torque with spherical ends) and were amassed in votive hoards. They tended to resurface after heavy rain, to the amazement of 18th-century peasants, who dubbed them "rainbow cups," imagining a link between these simultaneous apparitions.

"Rainbow cups" (left), plentiful in southern Germany in the 3rd century BC, were probably of more magical than economic value. Torques, groups of dots, and other decorative motifs composed a sacred grammar.

Secret Divinities

The Celts practiced nature cults devoted to the sky, stars, earth, hills, mountains, forests and clearings (even particular trees), rivers, lakes, the sea, and especially symbolic animals. A poem dating from the end of the 3rd century BC mentions the "jealous Rhine," to which the Celts would appeal for a verdict on the legitimacy of their offspring, while a Gallic chief, victorious in northern Italy, boasted of being the son of the Rhine River. Names also hint at these cults: tribal ones—the Eburones were the Yews and the Tarbelli the Bulls, or personal ones—Brannogenos, Son of the Crow, or Matugenos, Son of the Bear.

Brennus is said to have burst out laughing when he was told about the temple of Delphi and of how the Greeks believed the gods had human forms that they depicted in wood and stone. The Celts themselves were generally reluctant to make images of their gods. Though this situation may have been due to the influence of the druids, jealous guardians of contact with the gods, it also reflects an age-old taste for abstraction. However, after the Roman conquest, divine images quickly became very widespread. Later on, the legendary tales of the Celts of Britain teem with allusions to images of deities as they must have existed on the Continent.

The name of the deity on this late-1st-century BC limestone pillar statue found in a pit is not known. Its resemblance to a wooden sculpture suggests that this figure, wearing the torque symbolic of divinity, was probably often carved in wood.

Portraits of Bloodthirsty Gods

Some Gallic peoples are said to have appeased cruel gods Teutates and terrible Esus with hideous sacrifices. These seem to have been fearsome gods, with a thirst for human blood. Medieval texts tell of the sacrifices they were offered according to their tastes. For Teutates a man was drowned in a tub; for Esus one was hung from a tree and pulled to pieces; for Taranis several people were burned alive.

Caesar, in his *Commentaries on the Gallic War,* lists the deities worshiped by his enemies. He describes them by their Roman names: Mercury, inventor of the arts and protector of highways and trade; Apollo, who cures illnesses; Minerva; Jupiter; and so on.

Speaking of Mars, he adds that when a war began the Celts would dedicate to this god all the booty they might win, and that, having won, they would kill the living spoils and heap up the rest in a sacred place. Piles of miscellaneous booty could be seen in many communities, and it was very unusual for anyone to dare, for fear of the religious law, either to withhold his own takings or to lay a sacrilegious hand

Carved stones were found in 1711 under the Cathedral of Notre-Dame in Paris, having been reused to build a wall. One block bears a dedication to Jupiter made in Tiberius's reign by a guild of Gallo-Roman watermen. Another represents a god on each of its four faces: Jupiter, Vulcan, Esus, and Tarvos Trigaranus. The face with Esus (engraving, top left) is the only definite image known of this god.

upon the offerings: Such crimes would be punished with a terrible death. There was the same divine hierarchy in Ireland. Lug, surnamed Samildánach and armed with javelin and sling, was god of all the arts. Dagda, the good god, a fighter armed with a big club and lord of abundance with his inexhaustible cauldron, was surnamed Ollathair, father of all. Ogma symbolized physical strength, Dian Cécht was the physician god, and Goibniu the divine smith. The Welsh gods had the same functions but different names.

It has recently emerged that the Roquepertuse limestone statues were once covered in painted decoration. This sculpture (left), among the most important from southern Gaul, shows two heads with different faces joined back to back—like some Greek images of Hermes—and treated very realistically. It is a clear example of the influence of Hellenistic art on a society that had been steeped in Mediterranean culture for a long time.

Shared Beliefs

Apparent regional diversity conceals an underlying unity in Celtic mythology.

A Gallo-Roman bronze statuette around 8 inches high of Artio, goddess with a bear, was found at Muri, near Bern (Switzerland). She has sometimes been regarded as a remote ancestor of the town's emblem. Bears and wolves must have been plentiful in Celtic times, but few traces of them remain—apart from a few teeth in graves in Ardennes, a wooded region in northern France and Belgium.

This cauldron (left top) found at Gundestrup, in Denmark, in 1891 had been dismantled and deposited as a votive offering in a bog. It was probably made in the Balkans, on the eastern fringe of the Celtic world, much of whose mythology it brings together. Made of partially gilded silver, it is nearly 30 inches in diameter and dates from the 1st century BC. On the outside are seven panels bearing heads of more or less terrifying divinities (left center and bottom). The inside displays ritual scenes, in particular a whole procession, complete with musicians and sacrificial ceremonies. Cernunnos (opposite above) is represented sitting cross-legged with a ram-headed snake (symbol of earthly prosperity and aggressive force) in one hand and in the other a twisted torque of the same type that he wears around his neck. A helmeted female divinity (opposite below) is surrounded by exotic animals—a cat, elephants, and winged griffins—a very un-Celtic collection in which influence from the Black Sea can clearly be seen.

The triad is a recurrent symbol. There is also evidence of deep concern for the earth, sacred geography, frontiers, and natural configurations. Every distinctive feature of the landscape had a mythical significance.

The cult of Mercury covered vast areas of Europe. His indigenous name, Lug, recurs in about fifteen ancient place-names, including Lugdunum (Lyons) and Luguvalium (Carlisle). The great harvest festival Lugnasad was celebrated in all Celtic areas.

The goddesses Rosmerta, Nantosuelta, Damona, Sirona, Nemetona, and many others were partners of male divinities. It is not always easy to tell them apart from the *matres,* or *matronae,* divine mothers whose cult was deeply rooted in Celtic religious tradition. As mothers of the peoples they carried horns of plenty, baskets of fruit, and fertility symbols. The father god, Dispater, was great lord of the earth, and the Gauls claimed to be his descendants.

The cult of a divine smith corresponding to Vulcan is known by the name Goibniu in Ireland and Gofannon in Wales. Esus, a good god, though avid for human blood, is shown as a laborer and is associated with Tarvos Trigaranus, the bull with three cranes. The bull was a symbol of fertility and fighting strength. The stag, another fighting male, was the most prestigious wild animal: His antlers grow anew every year, a symbol of nature's cycle.

The Druids

Forming a privileged intellectual elite and masters of literature and poetry, the druids devoted about twenty years to their training, mostly memorizing

Tarvos Trigaranus, the bull with three cranes (top left), may be echoed in Irish epics: The hero Cú Chulainn pursued a divine bull, which was alerted by three goddesses in the form of crows. Cernunnos (above), the supreme god of Celtic forests, often appears wearing a torque; here bracelets hang from his antlers.

sacred texts. They were forbidden to write these down, though by Caesar's time the druids were literate. They were versed in mathematics, studied the movements of the stars, and claimed they could measure the universe. Mediators between humans and the gods, to whom they alone had access, they regulated religious ceremonies, presided at sacrifices, and interpreted omens. They taught that the soul does not perish after death but moves from one body to another or goes on living "elsewhere." This belief gave courage and helped overcome the fear of death.

In popular imagery, druids are often shown harvesting mistletoe. This was not only a magic ritual but an expression of deeper beliefs and worship of a great Celtic god connected with the natural cycle of the seasons. Mistletoe, a perennial plant, was to the tree what the soul was to the body, proceeding from the god, or even the god himself incarnate as a plant.

"The druids…consider nothing more sacred than mistletoe and the tree that it grows on, so long as it is an oak.… Below the tree they prepare a sacrifice and religious feast, and bring two white bulls whose horns are bound for the first time. A priest clad in white climbs the tree, cuts the mistletoe with a golden hook, and catches it on a white cloak. Victims are sacrificed with prayers to the god to render this offering propitious.…"

Pliny the Elder
(AD 23–79)
Natural History

h generatio
34

The valiant Celts of the Iron Age gave way before the combined onslaught of the Germanic tribes and the Romans. Nonetheless, throughout the first millennium AD, Celtic traditions were being worked into the background of early Christian art. It was especially in areas like Ireland and northern Scotland, which never came under Roman rule, that Celtic aesthetic styles flourished.

CHAPTER VI
CELTIC MEMORIES

The *Book of Kells,* a masterpiece of Celtic art created in c. 800 AD, contains the Latin gospels accompanied by Irish texts. This manuscript page (opposite) has such fine details that some are barely visible to the naked eye. Right: A statuette of a deity clasping a lyre from Paule, in northwestern France, made c. 70 BC.

Celtic society continued to evolve throughout its history, just as its geographical organization also changed. In Caesar's time Gaul was organized on the basis of a network of urban oppida, and each political grouping achieved stability through the institutions that were shared among the component tribal units. In pre-Christian Ireland, by contrast, tribal groups were widely scattered in small units around a rural landscape, and the king was the crucial symbol of unity and the bond with ancestral territory. The family, clan, kingdom, ties of blood, and the collective ownership of land were the organizing principles of a society that was archaic in comparison to continental models.

Christianity arrived in Ireland in the 5th century, spread by the famous missions of St. Patrick. The knowledge of Latin awakened interest in ancient culture. Ancient Celtic styles were reborn in the new Christian iconography and served as the inspiration for much manuscript illumination. Monumental carved stone crosses, reliquaries, shrines, and croziers following Celtic

designs were still being made in the 1100s. It was only after the Norman invasions of England in the 11th and 12th centuries and the arrival of new monastic orders from the Continent that Celtic art was supplanted by other models. Only in literature were its remnants preserved.

Old Irish Language and Legends

The first written texts go back to the 6th century AD. These are short, mainly funerary, inscriptions engraved in ogham (writing based on the Latin alphabet but shaped as lines or dashes). Later on, glosses inserted into 7th- to 9th-century Latin manuscripts allowed Old Irish to be identified and its grammar to be defined. It appears in books

The *Book of Durrow* (c. 675 AD, a page left) was written in the monastery at Durrow, reputedly by St. Columba himself. It contains four Latin gospels with translation and commentary. Its decoration drew upon a goldworking tradition that survived in Ireland until the 12th century and also influenced the style of Irish crosses (opposite), with a circle around the central motif that was to disappear with Romanesque art. Below: In solid gold and silver, the Irish Tara brooch (8th century AD) perfectly illustrates these Celtic artists' *horror vacui,* or dread of empty spaces.

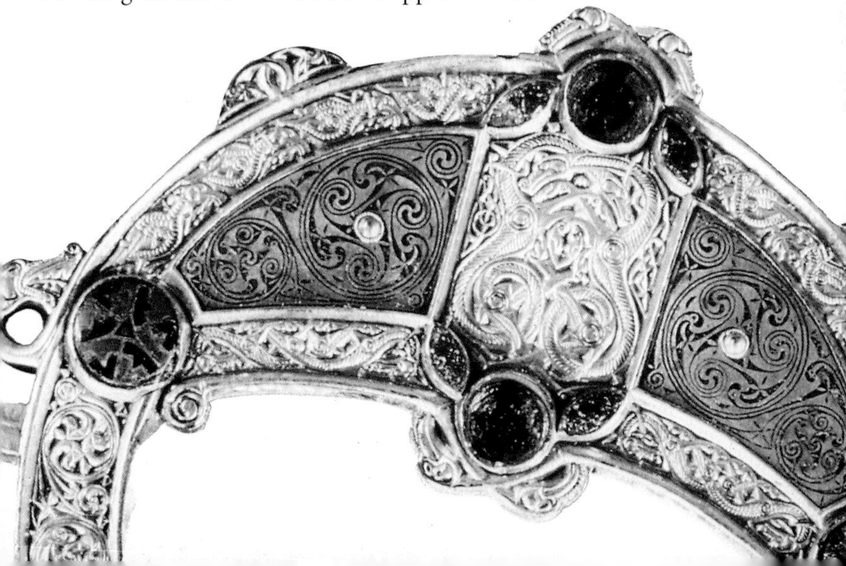

A gloss in tiny script was added in the 12th century to an 8th-century Irish manuscript (left). It is a legal text on the rights of women.

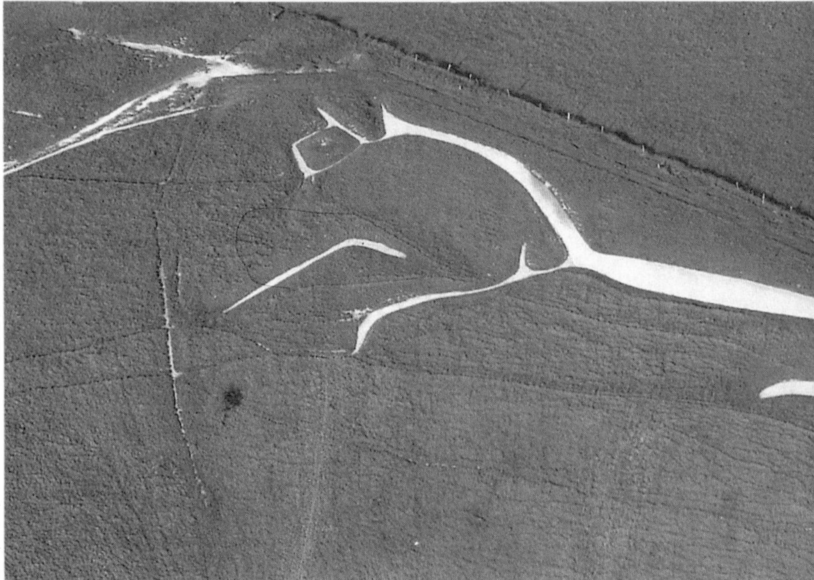

like the *Life of St. Columba,* the *Book of Kells,* and the *Book of Armagh.*

Legal texts written in Old Irish show concepts and procedures in force in Ireland in the 7th and 8th centuries. Welsh laws from the 10th century also survive.

Traditional tales were transcribed very early in Ireland. Poetry appeared in the 6th century, and narrative prose at the end of the 7th century. The exploits of heroes, legendary kings, and mythical figures were told in cycles: their conception and birth, their expeditions to the Otherworld, their

The huge white horse carved into the hillside at Uffington (Oxfordshire), near an Iron Age hillside fort, remains one of the great riddles of archaeology, since its design can be seen clearly only from the air. Normally ascribed to an early Celtic period, it may not have been made until the Middle Ages.

amorous adventures and battles, and, finally, their exemplary death. This heroic ideal corresponded closely to that of the continental Iron Age.

The Heroes of Irish Epic

One of the most famous epics is the Ulster Cycle. Its hero, Cú Chulainn, was the son of a divinity and died young but very gloriously. He did not care, he said, if he only lived a day and a night, so long as the tale of his exploits lived forever. He had a magic power that could rouse him to a frenzy. Hoping to calm him, his people once presented him with a hundred naked women, but he did not even see them. After killing many enemies he fell into a trance and was suffused with a radiance that was not to leave him until he died.

Another Irish cycle that also appeared in the 7th century had a profound influence upon European thought at the end of the Middle Ages —the Fenian Cycle. It draws on the Celtic tradition

Harpists were highly esteemed in Celtic society. Warriors gladly drew inspiration from the songs of poets who extolled their exploits. These epic tales spawned a tradition that has survived to this day: The songs of Ireland and Wales are still well known. Above: A 19th-century lithograph that reveals, with its freedom of interpretation, the Romantics' infatuation with the Celts.

of a band of warrior-huntsmen led by an extraordinary chief, Finn Mac Cumaill, who protected the kingdom from outside incursions. In Wales this theme was overlaid by the Arthurian legend, widely spread by oral tradition. This legend began to take shape in the 6th century, fueled by endless tales of wars with the Angles (a Germanic tribe that invaded Britain in the 5th century). The cauldron of plenty, supernatural objects, the heroes, and their adventures are all Celtic themes.

A popular 19th-century image (left) and a 1973 film version (above): The wicker man conjures up the cruel rites of the ancient Celts.

The Legacy of the Celts

Celtic languages declined during the Roman period, but they never actually stopped being spoken. Cornish disappeared in the 18th century, but modern Welsh, Armorican Breton, Irish, and Scottish Gaelic are very much alive today, and are even taught in schools. Few traces of ancient Celtic survive in English apart from words such as breeches (*bracae*) or bard (*bardos*). Celtic elements are common, however, in place-names: The Rhine relates to Celtic *renos* (raging flow) and Irish *rian* (sea), and place-names ending in -combe or -coomb are related to *cumba* (vase) or Welsh *cwm* (valley).

Celtic literary themes bridge

the centuries. The Arthurian cycle left a particularly rich legacy: King Arthur became a British national hero; in the 12th century the Normans took him to Sicily, and Chrétien de Troyes set his deeds to verse. In the 18th century James Macpherson had resounding success with *The Works of Ossian,* the stories of a bard who supposedly lived in the 3rd century AD.

Through music, songs, popular dances, and storytelling, Celtic traditions are still kept very much alive today and reinterpreted in an imaginative and vivid way.

In this 19th-century painting, *Ossian Receives the Souls of Heroes Who Died for Their Country,* by Anne-Louis Girodet, Napoleon Bonaparte enters into legend as a living hero. Overleaf: Detail of a 4th-century wine flagon handle from the tomb of the Waldalgesheim princess in Rhineland.

DOCUMENTS

From Strabo's descriptions to accounts of the Celts' resistance to Rome—a few fragments of what was once a civilization

The Celtic Lands on the Map of the Ancient World

The territory of the Celts—whom the Greeks called "Keltoi" and the Romans "Galli"—fluctuated over a large part of ancient Europe.

A 17th-century engraving of the Greek geographer Strabo.

Ancient Allusions to the Celts

According to descriptions given by Greek poets or Carthaginian explorers, Celtic homelands were dark, uninviting, and mysterious. At first both scholars and poets located the Celts vaguely to the west or north of the Mediterranean. But Greek poet Homer, in the 9th or 8th century BC, mentions areas farther west—and their populations—in the Odyssey.

We reached the deep-flowing ocean where the Cimmerians have their lands and their town. This people is hidden under clouds, in mists that the sun's bright rays have never pierced...a dismal night hangs over these unfortunates.

Homer
Odyssey, Book XI
9th or 8th century BC

The Land of the Hyperboreans

Greek legends recount that soon after his birth Apollo visited the Hyperboreans—a mythical people of the savage north—in a chariot drawn by swans. They locate this place "beyond the mountains, in lands of legend, where no compass points the way."

Hesiod, an 8th- or 7th-century BC Greek poet from Boeotia, referred to a river in the west as the "Eridanus with deep eddies," conceivably the Rhone. In his account of Hercules's voyage from the Isles of the Hesperides to Greece he alluded to what was later to become Gaul.

According to 5th-century BC Greek historian Herodotus, the "father of history," Aristeas, a mid-6th-century Greek poet, wrote an epic on the Arimaspeans in which he mentioned the Hyperboreans—the Celts?—in the far northwest of Europe.

Beyond the Issedones live the one-eyed Arimaspeans; gold-guarding griffins live beyond them; and then the Hyperboreans stretch to the sea.

Aristeas
quoted in Herodotus
Histories, Book IV
c. 425 BC

A century later the great Greek poet Pindar described the Hyperboreans as an ancient, sacred people, immune from illness, old age, fatigue, and war. There was, however, little exact knowledge of northern Europe in Greece at that time, as testified to by Greek historian and geographer Strabo (c. 63 BC–c. AD 24).

It was through ignorance of these [northern] regions that people invented the mythical Rhipaean Mountains and the Hyperboreans....

Strabo
Geography, Book VII
c. AD 17

First Mention of the Celts

Celtic lands were clearly named in the 6th century BC by Greek historian and geographer Hecataeus, who was born in around 548 BC in Miletus in Asia Minor. After extensive traveling he drew up a map of inhabited territories and wrote commentaries about them.

As for Herodotus, the vast area that he specified as belonging to the Celts between the source of the Danube (in southern Germany) and the Iberian Peninsula (Spain and Portugal) is indeed accurate, as present-day archaeology confirms. He had probably actually encountered the Celts, whose name he mentioned in connection with a trip he made to the shores of the Black Sea.

The river Ister rises among the Celts and the town of Pyrene and crosses the whole of Europe. And the Celts are beyond the Pillars of Hercules [two promotories at the eastern end of the Strait of Gibraltar], next to the Cynetes, who live furthest west of all the peoples of Europe.

Herodotus
Histories, Book II
c. 425 BC

Other Views of Celtic Territory

The notion that Celts inhabited western Europe is drawn mainly from accounts by seafarers who often described only coastal regions.

Himilco, an early 5th-century BC Carthaginian navigator instructed to reconnoiter the Atlantic coastline and the seas of northern Europe, gave terrifying descriptions of these places, which were later reworked by the Latin poet Avienus.

Himilco said he took four months to cross the ocean from the Pillars of Hercules to the Oestrymnides (either the islands off the coast of ancient Armorica or the British Isles) "on a sea that was sluggish and blocked with weed, in danger on shoals and surrounded by sea monsters." He said that west of the Pillars of Hercules the absence of wind and a perpetual fog made navigation impossible.

Were these descriptions of the dangers that he faced sincere or were they exaggerated to conceal the failure of his mission? Or were they meant to sow confusion about the trade route for tin that he was supposed to investigate?

Pytheas, a 4th-century BC navigator and astronomer of Greek origin, explored the Atlantic and the North Sea. He certainly reached the Baltic Sea and left an astonishing account of his ocean travels.

A Greek Geographer of the Conquest Period

With Strabo we get our first exact geographical description of Celtic territory. In his time it reached from the Rhine River in Germany to the British Isles.

After Iberia, we come to Celtic territory, which reaches eastward as far as the Rhine. Its entire northern edge is bathed by the British Channel, since the whole length of Britain runs parallel to and opposite Celtica for a distance of 5000 stades. The eastern boundary of Celtica is defined by the river Rhine, which runs parallel to the Pyrenees. Its southern boundary is formed partly by the Alps, at the point where they start to rise close to the Rhine, and partly by the Mediterranean Sea at the point that is called the Galatic gulf, where there are the famous cities of Massalia [Marseilles] and Narbo [Narbonne]. Opposite this gulf, but facing the other way, there is another gulf that is also called the Galatic gulf, but faces north and toward Britain. Here, Celtic territory reaches its narrowest point, for it forms an isthmus of less than 3000 but more than 2000 stades. Between [these two gulfs] there is a mountain ridge that runs at right angles to the Pyrenees, called Mount Cemmenos [the Massif Central]; this comes to an end in the midst of the plains of Celtica. The Alps, which are very high mountains, describe a curve whose convex side faces the same plains of Celtica and Mount Cemmenos, while its hollow side faces Ligurian territory and Italy.

Strabo
Geography, Book II
c. AD 17

In his *Geography* Strabo locates the territories of the western Celts between the northern Alps, the British Isles, and the Iberian Peninsula. The map below was drawn in 1933 from Strabo's descriptions.

Beyond the Pillars of Hercules

Inspired by reading Himilco's and Pytheas's accounts of their travels, Rufus Festus Avienus, a 4th-century AD Roman poet, worked their images of a wild and dangerous west into his own geographical poem, Ora Maritima.

Water washes into open land and the world is completely surrounded by it. The Atlantic gulf lies at the point where the deep sea leaves the ocean and opens out to form the Mediterranean. Here stand the town of Gades [Gadir], once called Tartessus, and the pillars of dogged Hercules, Abyla and Calpe: Calpe on the left and Abyla close to Libya; the fierce north wind rages against them, but they stand firm.

Here, too, the head of a promontory

[Brittany] juts out, called Oestrymnis in a bygone age. Most of the towering mass of its rocky summit faces into the warm south wind. Under this promontory's crest the Oestrymnian gulf spreads out…and contains the Oestrymnides, islands with broad plains and rich mines of tin and lead. The people here are powerful, proud, energetic and industrious, trading in everything. Their boats sail freely on this rough expanse of sea and the ocean teeming with monsters. They do not make hulls of pitch pine, nor do they shape wooden keels in the usual way; but, amazingly, they contrive their ships by stitching skins together and cross the open sea on leather.

It takes a boat from there two days to reach the Sacred Isle, so called by the ancients. This island [Ireland] in the midst of the sea is very large, mostly inhabited by Hibernian folk. Nearby, back in the opposite direction, is the island of the Albiones [Britain].

From the Oestrymnides, if boats dare venture into waters where the northern skies ice the breeze, they reach Ligurian land, now deserted because the Celts have repeatedly driven its people away. The exiled Ligurians, driven by fate as so often happens, ended up where they now are, in places bristling with scrub, with stony soil, steep rocks, and looming mountains thrusting skyward. For a long time the fugitives scratched a living from rock shelters, shunning the sea which they feared because of the ancient danger; then peace, leisure, and security made them more daring and encouraged them to descend from their high dwellings to the seaboard.

Rufus Festus Avienus
Ora Maritima
4th century AD

A Present-Day Archaeologist's View

Alain Duval, a contemporary expert on the Celtic world, describes the extent of Celtic territory at the height of its expansion.

The 3rd century BC marked the peak of Celtic expansion. The Celts then occupied a vast area stretching from the British Isles to the northern reaches of the Black Sea.

Two great regions can be distinguished within it: a western Celtic zone and an eastern Celtic zone. The latter, in contact with the Hellenistic world (and not simply through the raids that armed bands launched into Greece) but also in contact with eastern neighbors like the Dacians, is by far the richer and more dynamic of the two. In the western Celtic zone, the tribes that Caesar later mentioned took up their positions in the 3rd and early 2nd centuries BC. Some of these tribes represent what can already rightfully be called Gauls, and as a result France is referred to as Gaul.

In the north of Gaul and in England lived the Belgae (the Insular Belgae were called Britons). In the west of Gaul, the Gauls called themselves Armoricans. In the 2nd century BC some of the most powerful peoples of Gaul were the Senones, the Arverni of Auvergne, and the inhabitants of the vast region from Burgundy to the Swiss plateau, the Aedui and the Sequano-Helvetii. In Languedoc lived the Volcae. It is still not known whether they were part of the Arverni people or eastern Celts who migrated to Gaul.

Alain Duval
Celtic Art of Gaul
1989

Classic Portraits of Early Europeans

Over the centuries the Celts have been attributed with certain shared physical features or character traits, sometimes in stark contrast to the models that emerge from their own statues or from studying their skeletons. "The Celts have a cool, damp, white, and hairless skin" wrote Greek physician Galen in the 2nd century. He also averred, "The Celts do not have a perfectly proportioned body."

A Nordic Type?

Classical writers, neighbors, and contemporaries of the Celts rhapsodized about their white skin, their light-colored eyes and hair, and their powerful muscles. For Mediterraneans these people from the north were a constant source of amazement. This is how Roman poet Virgil (70–19 BC) summed up their physical appearance, as portrayed on a shield belonging to Aeneas, protagonist of Virgil's epic poem The Aeneid.

Their hair was of gold, their clothing was of gold and light stripes brightened their cloaks. Their milk-white necks had gold collars around them, a pair of Alpine spears glinted in each warrior's hands, and their bodies were protected by tall shields.

Virgil
The Aeneid, Book VIII
c. 20 BC

The Myth of the Blond Giant

Did ancient Romans and Greeks think of themselves as very small? At any rate the Celts' great vitality impressed them. The 1st-century BC Greek historian Diodorus Siculus wrote a history of the world in forty books, from its origins to the Gallic war, and left this vivid account of the Gauls.

The Gauls are tall, with moist white flesh; their hair is not only naturally blond, but they also make artificial efforts to lighten its color by washing it frequently in lime water. They pull it back from the top of the head to the nape of the neck.... Thanks to this

Left: A 6th-century BC stone statue from a burial mound.

treatment their hair thickens until it is just like a horse's mane. Some shave their beards, others let them grow moderately; nobles keep their cheeks clean-shaven but let their moustaches grow long until they cover their mouths.... They wear amazing clothes: tunics dyed in every color and trousers that they call *bracae* [breeches]. They pin striped cloaks on top of thick cloth in winter and light material in summer, decorated with small, densely packed, multicolored squares.

Diodorus Siculus
Historical Library, Book V
c. 50 BC

The Celtic Temperament

Strabo wrote a seventeen-volume description of Europe, Asia, Egypt, and Libya called Geography. *His observations about Gaul and the Gauls were quite accurate.*

The whole nation that is nowadays called Gallic or Galatic is war-mad, and both high-spirited and quick for battle although otherwise simple and not uncouth. Because of this, if the Gauls are provoked they tend to rush into a battle all together, without concealment or forward planning. For anyone who wants to outwit them they are therefore easy to deal with, since it is enough to provoke them into a rage by any means at all, at any time and in any place. It will then be found that they are willing to risk everything they have with nothing to rely on other than their sheer physical strength and courage. If gentle persuasion is used, however, they will readily apply themselves to useful things such as education and the art of speaking. Their strength is due partly to their size—for they are large—and partly to their numbers.... In addition to their simplicity and exuberance the Gauls have a propensity for empty-headed boasting and have a passion for personal ornamentation. They wear a lot of gold: They put golden collars around their necks and bracelets on their arms and wrists, while dignitaries wear dyed or stained clothing that is spangled with gold. Their vanity therefore makes them unbearable in victory, while defeat plunges them into deepest despair. Their thoughtlessness is also accompanied by traits of barbarity and savagery, as is so often the case with the populations of the north.

Strabo
Geography, Book IV
c. AD 17

A carving of a man's head, from the 2nd or 1st century BC in Bohemia.

A modern historian comments on Strabo's depiction of the Gauls.

It may be asked…what can be learnt of the spirit of the Celts, and here, fortunately, Classical authors are…able to throw some considerable light.

"The whole nation…is war-mad, and both high-spirited and quick for battle although otherwise simple and not uncouth." These few words by Strabo perfectly express the impression gained of the Celts as a living people from all the written sources.… Strabo makes it clear that his description applied to the time of Celtic independence before Roman rule, and it is well to remember that he, as well as Diodorus Siculus, and other writers, make extensive use of earlier authors who had been able to make personal observations of Celtic life. Personal bravery, amounting to recklessness on the battlefield, and, at home, hospitality and a strict code of etiquette towards visitors, shows the Celtic householder as comparable to, if not a better person than, many of his more historical successors in the European countryside. Against the general impression of high spirits, if not excitability, and the impermanence of concerted action, there must be set the evidence for individual responsibility, and duties within a well-defined social system. The love of bright colours, adornment, praise and entertainment, feasting and quarrelling, all have remained European foibles when conditions have allowed, and none would be more natural than amongst a rustic people dwelling in the temperate regions of Europe.

T. G. E. Powell
The Celts
1983

Arrian (c. 96–c. 180), a Greek who obtained Roman citizenship and compiled the works of the Stoic philosopher Epictetus (born c. AD *60), presents a calm and sober synthesis.*

The Gauls are tall and have a high opinion of themselves.

Arrian
Anabasis of Alexander, Book I
c. AD 160

Roman Mistrust

In a speech of 69 BC *in defense of the government of Transalpine Gaul, Roman statesman Cicero (106–43* BC*) warned the Romans to beware of the Gauls, whose behavior had made them unworthy of trust.*

These are the very people who once went to Pythian Apollo at Delphi, so far away from their homelands, in order to desecrate and plunder the whole world's oracle. These same people—so religious, so scrupulous testifying here in court—besieged the Capitol.… Do you think they are humble and submissive here today, in their cloaks and breeches?… Look at them, cheerful and arrogant, pouring into the Forum with a threat on their lips, trying to frighten us with the noise of their barbaric language.…

It would be a monstrous black mark and a disgrace upon this empire if news reached Gaul that Roman senators and *equites* had given a verdict to suit the whim of the Gauls, not because of the merits of their case but because they were intimidated by their threats.

Cicero
Pro M. Fonteio
69 BC

The Magic of Language

The development of the Celtic language and art of speaking was complex, and its evolution shows the dynamism of Celtic culture. Diodorus Siculus and modern historian John Sharkey discuss the Celts' speaking style.

In conversation the Gauls' speech is brief and enigmatic, proceeding by allusions and innuendo and often exaggerating to puff themselves up and put others down. They have a threatening, boastful, tragic manner, and yet their minds are sharp and not without aptitude for learning.

Diodorus Siculus
Historical Library, Book V
c. 50 BC

The Celts love style, and their admiration for eloquence is unbounded. The Greek writer Lucian, who was travelling around Gaul during the second century BC, described a charming symbolic scene. An old man, clad in a lion-skin, with a beaming smile, led a group of followers whose ears are attached to his tongue by thin gold and amber chains. They followed him eagerly, praised him and danced around him. The explanation that Lucian was given was that the old man, named Ogmios (an echo of the druidic Ogham), represented eloquence, for it grew with age, and was more powerful than brute strength, hence the lion-skin of Hercules.

John Sharkey
Celtic Mysteries: The Ancient Religion
1975

A 6th-century BC stone statue of a warrior from the Hirschlanden barrow in Germany.

Celtic Society and Private Life

Often rather biased, ancient accounts of the Celts suggest a rough people with simple customs. The richness of archaeological evidence gives a wholly different impression of Celtic life, one governed by laws, social structures, and a relatively strict morality.

A Caricature of Celtic Society

Polybius (200–120 BC), an admiring Greek historian of Roman affairs, visited Cisalpine Gaul himself. It seems, however, that the primitive culture he attributes to the Gauls was no more than a device to conceal distinct gaps in his knowledge.

They lived in unwalled villages without much furniture to spare; for as they slept on beds of straw and leaves and fed on meat and spent their time exclusively on warfare and agriculture, their lives were simple, and they did not have any crafts or sciences. Each man's wealth took the form of cattle and gold, since only these things could be taken with them anywhere as they moved around and be shifted to suit their convenience. They held comradeship in highest esteem, since the most feared and powerful among them were those who were thought to have the most attendants and retainers.

Polybius
Histories, Book II, c. 140 BC

Social Divisions

Roman general and statesman Julius Caesar (100–44 BC) described in detail in his Commentaries on the Gallic War *not only his military campaigns of 58–1 BC but also his impressions of Gaul's inhabitants—an interesting mixture of precise observation and wild interpretation.*

In the whole of Gaul there are only two classes of men who count for anything and are considered, for the common people are like slaves: They can do nothing on their own account and are

A 19th-century engraving of a Gallic family.

never consulted. Most of them, crushed either by debts and taxes or by the injustice of more powerful men, have handed themselves over into servitude to nobles who have assumed the same rights over them that masters have over slaves. The other two classes are the druids and the *equites* [knights or barons]. The former preside over religious matters, see to public and private sacrifices, and expound doctrines...[the latter are responsible for military affairs].

Julius Caesar
Commentaries on the Gallic War
Book VI, 51 BC

Twentieth-century historian Stuart Piggott, in his book The Druids, *explored the evidence for a common social order on the Continent and in the British Isles.*

The two main areas of the Celtic world significant in our enquiry into the druids, Gaul and Ireland, both provide evidence for the Celtic social order, which can be seen to have been essentially the same in both regions. The Irish vernacular sources show us a simpler and more rustic world than do the classical writers, particularly Caesar, describing Gaul, and this is consonant with the archaeological evidence for a higher degree of sophistication and technological achievement on the Continent. The major social units in Gaul were what are usually translated "tribes"—*ethne* in the Greek and *civitates* in the Roman writers—and these have specific names, the familiar Helvetii or Veneti, Aedui or Atrebates. Within these large tribal areas there would be *pagi*, smaller territorial or kinship units or "clans," and in Caesar's time there were impermanent and shifting political coalitions in which the more powerful tribes might have several others in a relation of client powers. By this time too what had been an original system of tribal chieftainships (or "kings") was being replaced by an annually elected magistracy in the Roman manner (a member of which was known as a *vergobretos*), or by the oligarchic rule of the council of elders originally responsible to the "king" (*rix*) whose position had to some extent at least been elective from within the choice presented by the dynastic families, and there had also been a separate war leader on occasion. A phrase in Tacitus suggests that a similar decline in chieftainship had taken place in Britain.... Below the king and the royal family, society in Gaul was tripartite, with two classes of landowning freemen, the knights or barons (*equites*) from whom the council of elders was chosen, and the priesthood or clerisy, including *druides.* This learned class comprised not only druids, but bards (*bardoi*), and seers or diviners (*vates* or *manteis*), and probably other unnamed functionaries. Below these representatives of church and state came the unfree and landless men, the *plebes.* There was an internal grading in power and position among the "knights," and it seems that they did not constitute a closed caste, and some social mobility seems to have been possible. The druid and allied religious elite was equally not a caste, but open to entry from outside, from the class of *equites.*

The evidence from the law-tracts and hero-tales of Archaic Irish... shows that the normal area of the tribe (*túath*) ruled by a "king" (*rí*) was not comparable with the Gaulish *civitas,* but with the *pagus....*

On a lower and more primitive scale, "kingship" was universal in Ireland, elective from within the dynasty. Below the king came the landowning "grades of nobility"—the Gaulish *equites*—and between them and the freemen commoners came those of exceptional gifts of skill, the *aes dána* or "men of art"; expert craftsmen in things, word and thought, blacksmiths and bronze-workers, lawyers and genealogists, poets and musicians. In the Irish scheme of things druids designated as such are not normally in the dominant position the Gaulish (or at least Caesar's) evidence implies, but are contained within the men of art who were the men of learning, and also included the *filid* who were at once seers and wise men, and the repositories of the oral traditions not only of myth, legend, and family history, but of the formalized language and techniques of prosody in which these were preserved and transmitted, and the jurists responsible for customary law. There was a council of nobles, and a general assembly of the freemen of the tribe.... We see then a common pattern of society well documented in Gaul and Ireland, and by inference present elsewhere in the Celtic world.

Stuart Piggott
The Druids, 1975

Marriage and Death

Caesar recounts Celtic rights and rituals.

When men marry they receive a dowry from their brides, and to this they add a sum from their own possessions that is agreed as equivalent in value after an assessment; they keep a single account of this money and preserve all the interest on it. When one of them dies, the surviving spouse receives both portions together with the accumulated increase. Husbands have rights of life and death over their wives and children. Whenever a highborn head of family dies, his relatives assemble and, if there is anything suspicious about his death, wives are interrogated like slaves. If found guilty, they are put to death by fire after every sort of cruel torment. By Gallic standards their funerals are magnificent and sumptuous; everything

A Gallic banquet.

they think the dead man cherished in his lifetime is put on the pyre, even his animals; and also, not long before living memory, at properly conducted funerals the slaves and clients who had been dear to him were burnt along with him.

Julius Caesar
Commentaries on the Gallic War
Book VI, 51 BC

Status of Women

According to both an ancient and a modern historian, the Celts took a surprisingly progressive view of women and their capabilities.

The women of the Gauls are not only like men in their stature but they are a match for them in courage as well.

Diodorus Siculus
Historical Library, Book V, c. 50 BC

It is generally assumed that the right of a wife to hold independent property, or of a daughter to inherit, is a late development appearing in parallel form in different Indo-European legal systems. On the other hand, a more liberal, but still common, practice seems to have been operative at very varying dates as illustrated in Aryan, Roman and Celtic legal custom. There is also the question of the very rich Celtic women's graves, as at Vix and Reinheim, to take but two recently discovered examples. Here women, buried singly, had been accorded the most splendid funerary chambers, and the most sumptuous adornment and accessories. Personal prestige and the right to possess property may account for such instances, while all the considerations taken together seem to suggest that incapacity of women was a reflection of primitive conditions, predominant in times of migration or hardship, though the legal system was always sufficiently elastic in periods of prosperity, from place to place, to permit greater female freedom in public and family interests.

T. G. E. Powell
The Celts, 1983

Homosexuality

Diodorus Siculus noticed that, among the Celts, homosexuality was both common and expected.

Despite the fact that their wives are beautiful, the Celts have very little to do with them, but instead abandon themselves to a strange passion for other men. They usually sleep on the ground on skins of wild animals and tumble about with a bedfellow on either side. And what is strangest of all is that, without any thought for a natural sense of modesty, they carelessly surrender their virginity to other men. Far from finding anything shameful in all this, they feel insulted if anyone refuses the favors they offer.

Diodorus Siculus
Historical Library, Book V, c. 50 BC

Strange Customs

Diodorus Siculus gives the following colorful account of the Balearic Islanders, another warrior people with whom the Celts were often associated as mercenaries in Mediterranean armies.

At wedding feasts relatives and friends take it in turn to lie with the bride in order of age from eldest downwards, first to last. The bridegroom is the last to receive this honor. Their funeral rites are also conducted in a singular way: They break up the corpse's limbs with wooden implements and put it into a vat that they then cover with a heap of stones. Their weapons consist of three slings: one that they carry around their heads, another around their waist, and a third in their hands. In battle they can sling larger stones than anyone else, and with such force that they seem to have been shot by catapult. During assaults on strongholds they hit and disable defenders on the battlements, and in pitched battle they puncture shields, helmets, and all the enemy's defensive armor. And they aim so accurately that they very seldom miss their target. This is because they start practicing from early childhood, when even their mothers force boys into constant use of the sling. They put some bread on a post as their goal, and the children go hungry until they hit the bread and get their mother's permission to eat it.

Diodorus Siculus
Historical Library, Book V, c. 50 BC

Feasts

Posidonius (1st century BC) was the first Greek writer to visit the interior of Gaul. He made an interesting ethnographic study of the Celts.

Sometimes the Celts fight duels during their feasts. Though they are always armed at these gatherings, they engage in mock combat and spar among themselves with fists; they still sometimes end up with wounds, and then, becoming angry, if bystanders do not separate them, they go on to get killed.... In former times, when the hindquarters were served, the bravest man claimed the best cut, and if someone else wanted it, the two contestants stood up and fought to the death....

When many people dine together they sit in a circle, with the most important man in the central place, like the leader in a chorus; this is someone who excels the others by virtue of his martial skill, birth, or wealth. Next to him sits the host, and then alternately on either side come all the others, in order of rank. Their shield-bearers stand behind them, and the spearsmen sit in front in a circle like their lords and feast in common in the same way. The servants take the drink around in ceramic or silver vessels that look like spouted cups; the dishes on which the food is arranged are made of the same materials or sometimes of bronze or are wooden or wicker baskets. The drink served to the rich is wine imported from Italy or Massaliote territory: They drink it neat or sometimes mixed with a little water; the less well-off drink a wheaten beer brewed with honey; the common people drink it plain.

Posidonius
Histories, Book XXIII, c. 70 BC
quoted in Athenaeus
The Deipnosophists, Book IV, c. AD 200

The Celtic Heroic Tradition

Celtic heroism and desire for immortality is discussed by two present-day writers.

The heroic ethos of the Celts, as of many other peoples, is neatly epitomized in the words of the Irish hero Cú Chulainn: "Provided I am famous, I do not care whether I live but a single day in this world." In such a society, in which life—and individual status—was dominated by an extremely sensitive regard for personal honour, it was essential that one should earn the respect of one's peers and, especially, of those poets, seers and learned men whose responsibility it was to shape and to interpret the mythology, the laws and the historical traditions of the tribal community.

Proinsias MacCana
"Celtic Heroic Tradition," *The Celts*
1991

To be a warrior among warriors was the ideal life for the Celt, but to die in a fight surrounded by friends, poets and a hundred dead enemies was the supreme consummation.... The preparation for the supreme moment, from his initiation onwards, gave the Celtic warrior his fearlessness and pride. Such qualities were noticed and commented upon by all the classical Greek and Roman

This iron firedog and frame, possibly used for holding wine amphorae, was found in a grave with other provisions for feasting.

writers, who also refer to the Celts' love of fighting and easy attitude to death. In the Cú Chulainn story, the sun god materializes to take over the functions of the warrior, who by dying for three days can remain mortal. In this bardo state [between dying and being reborn] he can ascend the three mystical worlds of the Celtic after-life: from earth-body to the physical spirit and finally into the radiant soul-light in which the sun himself is manifest. When Cú Chulainn sleeps he becomes joined to his own embodied radiance, inhabiting all worlds at once. This easy movement between the human warrior hero and his other-worldly archetype, the sun god, is a common practice in every kind of Celtic story. This is the key to the Celtic Mysteries—the merging of the spiritual, physical and imaginative planes.

John Sharkey
Celtic Mysteries: The Ancient Religion
1975

Languages and Writing in Celtic Culture

There were not one but several Celtic languages, and all belong to the Indo-European group. None, however, seems to have used its own alphabet. Celtic inscriptions used borrowed alphabets that the Celts adapted. We have medieval Irish monks to thank for the preservation of Celtic literature, passed on to them by oral tradition.

Language as Social Evidence

The next point to be clarified is how it can be shown that the Celts of antiquity actually spoke tongues related to the surviving languages that in philological terminology are described as Celtic. This can be most readily demonstrated through the classics in the names of chieftains and tribes, and particular words or terms recorded as belonging to the Celts. This body of linguistic material falls within the Celtic branch of the Indo-European language family, and in many cases the anciently recorded words can be shown to have survived into the medieval and modern languages of the Celtic group.

There are three other primary sources on the language of the ancient Celts. In the first place there is the existence of a large number of inscriptions incorporating Celtic words and names, but mainly written in Latin, or more rarely in Greek. These were inscribed on altars and other monuments in the Celtic regions incorporated within the Roman Empire, and they have been found from as far apart as Hadrian's Wall and Asia Minor, Portugal and Hungary. The second source is akin. It is numismatic, but much more restricted in space. It is particularly valuable on account of coins inscribed with names, linguistically Celtic, that can be shown on archaeological and historical grounds to have been issued by Celtic kings or tribes. The third line of evidence has to do with place-names. These are as often river or other topographical names as those of actual settlements or strongholds.

A direct link can be established in many cases through the classics in reference to the Celts, but the distributional evidence of Celtic place-names in Western and Central Europe conforms closely with the regions in which the Celts are known to have been strongest, and in which their influence lasted longest.

T. G. E. Powell
The Celts
1983

The Diversity of Celtic Languages Mirrors the Variety of Celts

The languages spoken by Celtic peoples today belong to two groups: Brythonic (or P-Celtic) and Goidelic (or Q-Celtic).... The Goidelic dialects include Irish, Gaelic (spoken in the west coasts of Scotland) and Manx; while Welsh, Cornish and Breton belong to the Brythonic branch. This distribution is the result of the migrations of the 5th and 6th centuries AD.... The migration of the Irish westward introduced the Goidelic dialect into the western parts of Scotland, where it became known as Gaelic, and into the Isle of Man; while Brythonic remained in use in Wales and Cornwall and was carried to Brittany by the folk movements from Devon and Cornwall in the 5th and 6th centuries. The Irish form of Celtic remained dominant in Ireland...until the 16th century, when English began to take over. But in Scotland the Celtic language had begun to be replaced by English somewhat earlier. In the Isle of Man, Manx was spoken extensively in the 17th century but has died out, apart from its use on ceremonial occasions. In Cornwall, too, Celtic expired in the 18th century, but in Brittany it has remained. Today about half of the population can speak Breton. Celtic can be heard widely throughout western Ireland though hardly at all in Ulster, while in Scotland only fifteen per cent of the population are Gaelic speaking, but they are concentrated in the Hebrides. In Wales, however, twenty-six per cent of the population speak Welsh.

Barry Cunliffe
The Celtic World
1986

The Message Carried by the Language

The Celts of the extreme West—Bretons, Scots, Welsh and Irish—are today the sole guardians of the memory of the ancient Celtic peoples.... It is they who have preserved the legacy of an original literature, the work of

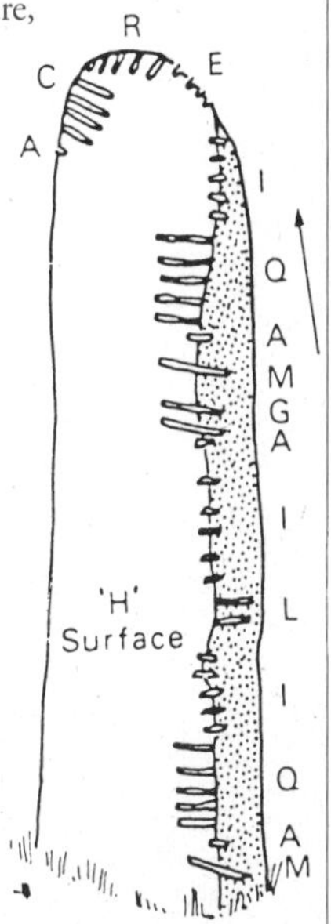

The number and position of lines carved on either side of the stone's edge allow characters in ogham script to be identified. On the page opposite is the Castlekeeran stone (Ireland).

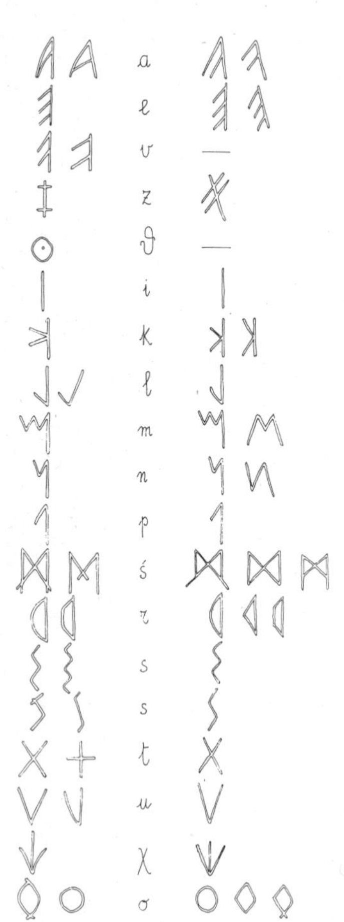

Celtic incriptions in the Lepontic alphabet appeared very early in northern Italy. Above: The alphabet used in the 6th century BC. Right: The alphabet of the 2nd and 1st centuries BC used on the Iberian Peninsula.

generations of anonymous poets, already several centuries old when it was written down by Irish monks in the early Middle Ages. The Insular Celts, last bearers of an oral tradition that, in other lands with a Celtic past, dispersed into the luxuriant world of folk legend, have kept alive a representational tradition that is as important as epic and mythological tales in the cultural treasure left to us by the peoples of ancient Europe....

Increasing weight is given today to one particular category of archaeological evidence: the texts, unfortunately short and very few, that the ancient Celts wrote in their own language with the help of various alphabets borrowed from the Mediterranean world....

The Celts emerge around the end of the 4th century BC from the anonymity of the ancient European peoples who had no writing. Their linguistic family, which had split off from early Indo-European nearly

Above: A 2nd- or 1st-century BC stone slab with Gallo-Greek inscriptions, from Vaison-la-Romaine, in southeastern France.

two millennia previously, had a long history behind it at this time and was divided into several distinct groups that occupied vast areas of western central Europe....

However, analysis of so-called Lepontic inscriptions, composed at the end of the 6th century BC in characters derived from the Etruscan alphabet, indicate that Celtic groups, the first to make use of writing to record their language, were already well integrated into northern Italy—in present-day Lombardy and perhaps further south—when their Transalpine cousins came to settle in the Po valley and descended upon Rome.

Venceslas Kruta
The Western Celts
1955

Were the Celts Bloodthirsty Warriors?

Ancient authors stressed the courage and cruelty of the Celts as a way of paying tribute to the brave warriors who dared to confront them. These fierce, half-naked combatants were at a clear disadvantage against the Romans because of the nature of their equipment and their lack of organization.

Fearless Combatants

By all accounts the Celts do not appear to have been a passive people.

All the Galatae [Celts], the Triballi [Thracians], and many other barbarians believe in the soul's immortality, so they have no fear of death and go out to embrace danger.

Iamblichus
Life of Pythagoras, Book XXX, c. AD 300

The Celts changed the conventional methods of warfare of the first millennium BC with their large iron hacking swords, their spear-throwing from fast two-horsed chariots, and their use of screaming naked riders to create terror and confusion.

John Sharkey,
Celtic Mysteries: The Ancient Religion, 1975

Head-hunters

Diodorus Siculus here alludes to a Celtic practice whose historical reality has never been absolutely proven.

When [the Celts] kill enemies in battle they cut off their heads and attach them to the necks of their horses. They leave the other bloody remains to their servants to carry off as plunder, sing hymns of praise and victory songs, and finally nail these first-fruits to their houses, as people do with wild animals after certain kinds of hunting. They soak the heads of their most illustrious enemies in cedar oil and keep them

Left: A helmet from Casino Pallavicino, Italy. Opposite: A Celtic warrior holding the head of an enemy.

carefully in a chest and show them off to strangers, each priding himself that for one or other of these heads either a forebear, or his father, or he himself had refused to take a large sum of money. Some are said to boast that they have even refused its weight in gold for one of these heads, thereby displaying a barbaric sort of magnanimity, for there is nothing noble in refusing to sell the proofs of one's valor.

Diodorus Siculus
Historical Library, Book V, c. 50 BC

The Terrible Carnage at Telamon During the Second Punic War

In 225 BC a coalition of Cisalpine Gauls, reinforced by Transalpine mercenaries, the Gaesatae, met the forces of Rome in a decisive battle at Telamon, on the coast of northern Etruria. Polybius described it, probably following the eyewitness account recorded by Quintus Fabius Pictor, a Roman historian who served in the war.

The Insubres and Boii entered battle wearing breeches and with light cloaks wrapped around them, but the Gaesatae, in their presumptious self-assurance, had thrown off their clothes and took up position in the first rank, naked apart from their weapons, thinking they would fight better that way.… The first engagement took place on the hill.… Cavalry from both armies milled around.… Then, when the infantry troops made contact, there was a unique and extraordinary encounter. … A din arose from countless horns and war-trumpets, and such a loud clamour of war-cries broke from the whole army in concert that not only the trumpets and soldiers but even the surrounding countryside itself reverberated with echoes and seemed

to be giving voice. Terrifying, too, were the appearance and movements of the powerful naked men at the front, all in the prime of life. The men in the front lines were decked out with collars and bracelets of gold. The Romans then had a double incentive to fight, on the one hand horrified by what they saw before them, but also eager to win spoils.

When the [Roman] soldiers.… unleashed a dense shower of javelins upon them, their cloaks and breeches provided very useful protection for the Gauls in the rear, but for the naked men in front things turned out very differently from what they had expected, causing them much confusion and suffering. For the Gaulish shield is unable to cover the whole body, so the more naked they were and the larger their bodies were, the easier the javelins found it to hit their uncovered parts. Finally, unable to counterattack their assailants because of the distance between them and the rain of javelins, badly battered and sorely tried by the situation, some perished by launching themselves blindly upon their enemies in a fit of mindless rage and thereby going to a deliberate death, while others disorganized the ranks behind them by retreating backwards step by step and letting them see their terror. In this way the pride of the Gaesatae was broken under the impact of the javelins, but once the Romans had opened their ranks to withdraw their marksmen and instead launched their maniples against [the Gauls], the mass of the Insubres, Boii and Taurisci rushed headlong into the enemy and engaged in a violent hand-to-hand battle. Riddled though they were with wounds, they kept up equal spirits with the Romans but were collectively and individually disadvantaged by one thing—the nature of their equipment. Their shields gave far inferior protection, while their swords were far less effective in attack, since the Gaulish sword can only slash. When the Roman cavalry descended from the heights and charged vigorously from the flank the Celtic infantry was cut to pieces where it stood and the cavalry took flight.

Polybius
Histories, Book II, c. 140 BC

Chariot Tactics

The lightly built Celtic war chariots combined speed and maneuverability. Their onslaughts were dreaded.

This is what [British] chariot warfare is like. First of all they drive about in every direction hurling their javelins: the fear engendered by the horses and the din of the wheels is usually enough to disorder the enemy ranks. Then they slip between the squadrons of cavalry and leap off their chariots to fight on foot. Meanwhile the chariot drivers gradually withdraw from the battle and position the chariots in such a way that if the fighting men are overwhelmed by enemy numbers they can quickly return to them. They therefore combine the mobility of cavalry with the solidity of infantry in battle, and [the Britons] become so skilled in their use through training and daily practice that they can even control galloping horses on steep and dangerous inclines, make them slow down very quickly, and turn them around; they themselves can also dart out forwards along the shaft, stand steady on the yoke, and then return in a flash back to their chariots.

Julius Caesar
Commentaries on the Gallic War
Book IV, 51 BC

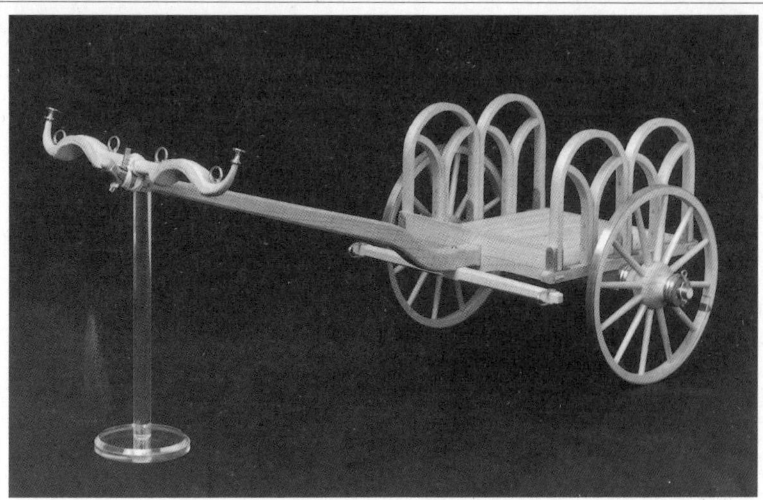

A reconstruction of a British war chariot (above). An early Gallic coin depicting a chariot scene (opposite).

The initial purpose of the chariot warrior was to drive furiously towards and along the front of the enemy ranks to instil terror by sight, and by the delivery of missiles, no less than by the tremendous noise that was kept up by shouting, horn blowing, and beating on the sides of the wagons drawn up to the flanks or in the rear. The warriors then descended from their chariots, which the charioteer held in readiness for a quick retreat if need be, while the warrior, with casting spear, or drawn sword, stood out to deliver a challenge to an opposing champion. The challenge was evidently in a set formula of boasts of prowess, and perhaps of lineage, incorporated in a war song. Indeed, a kind of frenzy was probably worked up. In inter-tribal fighting, it would appear that the main body of troops became involved only after this phase of individual contest, and perhaps only if one side had become certain of success in a general mêlée. The course of events against Roman armies must have involved the whole body of fighting men more directly, and it led to considerable modifications in battle order.

T. G. E. Powell
The Celts, 1983

Celtic Warriors on Horseback

At the time of the Roman conquest the Gauls preferred cavalry battles to other types of warfare. But these were not the tactics they had used in earlier times.

Like the Greeks and Latins, the Celts and Belgae embarked upon the art of war with chariot combat. Contact with Mediterranean armies led the Italian and eastern Celts to give up this old practice. It disappeared more slowly from Gaul and Britain, where some peoples doggedly preserved their ancestors' ancient weapon.... In Celtica proper, territory of the Arverni and Aedui, by the end of the 2nd century BC the war chariot had been reduced to no more than ceremonial use, a vehicle for processions or triumphs, as it had become and was to remain in republican Rome. Among the Belgae, by contrast, who had coalesced more recently and lived further away from civilized armies, it was regularly used as a fighting vehicle for a longer period, and there were some Belgic peoples, perhaps including the Remi, who stuck to it as though it were a defining feature of their identity.... Besides, it was not a bad way to fight: Chariots carried a driver and a soldier on two wheels. Being very light, they reached the enemy quickly: Standing upright, with the advantage of extra height, and close enough not to miss his target, the warrior would throw his lance or javelin and then withdraw at speed, or, if he preferred, get down to use his sword....

But noble Gauls in Caesar's time preferred to fight on horseback. There had doubtless once been a time when a horse served a warrior not primarily as a mount but as a vehicle, by which I mean that it afforded a way of reaching the battlefield more quickly, where the rider then fought on foot: horse-riding did no more than simplify the role of the war chariot. However, the war-horse was by now a fighting instrument, if I may so describe it. The terms "cavalry" and "aristocracy," "horseman," and "noble" became if not synonymous, at least inseparable....

All other weapons, especially in Celtic environments, seem to have been subordinate to the noble weapon, the sword, the weapon of close contact: just as, of all martial displays cavalry processions were preferred. The true Celtic warrior was therefore a horseman of battles and skirmishes, charging and slashing.

Celtic Swords: Long and Cumbersome

For attacking, the Gauls discovered the most suitable weapon for horsemen or tall foot soldiers: a blunt-ended long iron sword, wide, flat, tapering, and double-edged, which allowed a strong arm swinging it from high on horseback to slash into or fell an adversary's body. The Celts were attached to these weapons; they forged enormous

Bronze sculpture of a Gallic horseman.

numbers of them for their multitudes, and it was probably because of them that they so often settled in iron-bearing areas of Europe and became the main agents for spreading the new metal at the expense of bronze. The large sword may have ensured them victory over various Ligurian or Illyrian populations of central Gaul, still with little experience of contact weapons; its cutting strength must have been largely responsible for the initial agitation of the southern world, which was only familiar with short, stabbing swords. A true cavalry saber, the Celtic weapon seems to have had the double advantage of keeping the enemy at a distance while also reaching them.

But the Gauls' adversaries quickly discovered the shortcomings of this formidable instrument. To counter its dangerous edge the Romans reinforced the armour plating of their shields and helmets, and the Gaulish sword, soft and poorly tempered, bent with the first blows. It could not thrust: To disarm it, Latin soldiers had only to be armed with long spears. Heavy and cumbersome, it was difficult for an arm to wield it fast and accurately.... It was a very easy matter for a forewarned adversary to avoid such blows; the barbarian's weapon then fell into thin air and he himself was left shaken and demoralized by the futile effort he had made, unable to respond to a reasonably active counter-attack. These swords resembled their masters: Like them, they were made for display and were doomed to crumple.

Camille Jullian
History of Gaul, 1920

A decorated sword found at Tesson, in western France.

The Manufacture of Blades

It seems possible that some of the [swords] may...represent a regional style of manufacture, rather than the result of complex trading patterns, pilgrims depositing objects from far afield, travelling smiths or locally based craftsmen trained elsewhere, or any combination of these possibilities.

What is certain is that there were several major innovative centres of the ironsmiths' art in eastern Europe, particularly in Hungary. But both to east and west of this region there were other local workshops and artistic variants of the armourers' art, sharing certain motifs such as the dragon pair, the birds' heads and vegetal patterns. These frequently have distributions well beyond their original area of development, though this may be due not so much to trade alone as to the constant journeyings of professional warriors and even craftsmen.

Ruth and Vincent Megaw,
Celtic Art: From Its Beginnings to the Book of Kells, 1989

The Druids

Druids were at the apex of a religious hierarchy that included soothsayers and bards. After a long and strict initiation they joined an elite that held power and knowledge. Their concerns were theology, morals, and legislation as well as astronomy and divination.

A Spiritual Identity

Given the diversity and frequent inadequacies of our sources it would be unrealistic to expect from them a clear image of a unified, consistent order of religious belief. Nowhere have we the integral tradition as it might have been transmitted and interpreted by the druids and their associates in an independent Celtic society. No source or group of extant sources was designed to furnish an ordered, comprehensive picture of native religion as seen from within its own cultural community. The effect of this has been to accentuate the heterogeneity of Celtic religion, and it has sometimes led scholars to exaggerate its local and tribal character

The druids' grove. A stage set for *Norma,* an opera written by Vincenzo Bellini in 1831.

and to ignore the many features which reflect the underlying unity of Celtic myth and ritual.... There were in fact individual gods whose cults extended over all, or over large parts of, the Celtic areas of Europe. "Mercury," the most widely venerated of the Gaulish gods according to Caesar, is a case in point.

Proinsias MacCana
"Celtic Religion and Mythology"
The Celts, 1991

The idea that the ancient Celts had a common religion is based on comparative inferences from the corpus of records on Indo-European religions in our possession, and on iconographic studies made on La Tène art. It is actually impossible to establish any relationship, other than speculative, between these two sets of documentation. Furthermore, the same difficulties are encountered when attempting to draw parallels between the portraits of Gallo-Roman deities and those presumed to be from the La Tène pantheon. The reason for these difficulties probably lies in the basic incompatibility of the two systems of figurative expression.

Unlike most ancient religions, Celtic religion cannot have comprised a consistent and unchanging set of beliefs. It must have been a composite pantheon of tribal gods, local deities (often pre-Celtic), and cults pertaining to specific social classes, all bundled together in a flexible system organized around a handful of major pan-Celtic gods from a common mythological "pool." Something of this pool has filtered down through medieval Irish and Gaulish literature, precious vestiges of an oral tradition which continues to thrive on the islands, a tradition that the advent of Christianity freed from the prohibition of written records.

Venceslas Kruta
"Celtic Religion"
The Celts, 1991

The Origins of the Word Druid

The word druid as used in modern European languages is derived from continental Celtic through Greek and Latin texts. Caesar for instance writes of *druides,* and Cicero of *druidae.* These, of course, are Latinized forms in the plural. In the surviving Insular Celtic languages, *druí* (sing.), *druad* (plur.) are forms of the same word from Old Irish texts. *Dryw* is the Welsh equivalent in the singular. Druid, as a word, is considered to derive from roots meaning "knowledge of the oak," or possibly "great, or deep, knowledge." Pliny [AD 23–79] compared the word to the Greek one for an oak tree.... The connection between the druids and the oak is indeed explicit in Pliny's account of the cutting of mistletoe from an oak tree by the druids, and the accompanying sacrifice of bulls. It is unfortunately unknown if this rite was connected with a tribal festival and for what purpose it was carried out. The oak groves at Olympia may also have been in Pliny's mind, and these certainly appear to have been a surviving Indo-European element in Greek cult comparable to the Celtic sacred woods, more particularly with the oak sanctuary (*Drunemeton*) of the Galatians. If the oak...was the symbol of deity, "knowledge of the oak" would be apposite for those who mediated with the supernatural.

T. G. E. Powell
The Celts, 1983

On Mistletoe

We must not forget the high regard in which the Gauls hold this plant. The druids (which is what they call their magicians) consider nothing more sacred than mistletoe and the tree that it grows on, so long as it is an oak. They select oak groves for the sake of that tree and will not perform any religious ceremony without its leaves. In fact the name "druid" can even be derived from the word "oak" if one employs a Greek etymology [*drys,* oak]. They think that anything that grows on an oak has been sent from heaven and treat it as a sign that the god himself has chosen that tree. Mistletoe is actually very rare on oak trees, and when it is found, it is culled with great ceremony. In the first place, the collection must take place on the sixth day of the moon. This day is the beginning of their months, their years, and their centuries (the latter last thirty years), and is a day on which the moon is already at full strength but is not yet in mid course. They give mistletoe a name that means cure-all.... Below the tree they prepare a sacrifice and religious feast and bring two white bulls whose horns are bound for the first time. A priest clad in white climbs the tree, cuts the mistletoe with a golden hook, and catches it on a white cloak. Victims are sacrificed with prayers to the god to render this offering propitious to the people who are making it. They believe that mistletoe in a drink confers fertility upon any sterile animal and is an antidote to all poisons. Such superstitious faith do people generally place in frivolous objects.

Pliny the Elder
Natural History, Book XVI, c. AD 77

Mystery, Doctrine, and Priesthood

The druid was shaman, priest, poet, philosopher, physician, judge and prophet. His initiation included several intermediate stages. Thus, the course of study for an Irish bard or *fili* included verse forms, composition and recitation of tales, the study of grammar, ogham, philosophy and law. The next seven years were for more specialist studies and included the secret language of the poets as the *fili* became an *ollamh*. He

A 19th-century depiction of druids on an island near the northwest coast of France.

could then acquire the knowledge of genealogy, and the committal of events and laws into poetic forms to become a doctor of law. Finally the "man of learning" would be fit to study incantations, divination and magical practice. "Thus every druid a bard, though every bard did not aspire to be a druid."

Caesar, describing the priesthood of Gaul, divides them into three groups: "The vates practised soothsaying and studied natural philosophy. The bards celebrated the brave deeds of their gods in verse. The druids were concerned with divine worship, the due performance of sacrifices, both private and public, and the interpretation of ritual questions." Their power seemed to be absolute, for in his observations the hardest penalty that could be levied on a person or family was exclusion from the sacrifices.

John Sharkey
Celtic Mysteries: The Ancient Religion
1975

Druids gathering sacred mistletoe.

The Role of the Druids

Within the larger Celtic community of Western Europe (never more than a patchwork of loose confederations), the druids were the custodians of vision and prophecy, sacrifice, poetic lore, the ritual calendar and the law—all the elements which united the different groups. The ritual traditions they maintained were oral ones.

John Sharkey
Ibid.

In the classical sources in the Posidonian group, on which we may place most reliance, the druids appear to have three main functions. In the first place they are the repositories of the traditional lore and knowledge of the tribe, whether of the gods, the cosmos and the other-world, or of the corpus of customary law and such practical skills as calendrical expertise. This body of knowledge was preserved in oral tradition (and probably mainly in verse form for mnemonic reasons) and continuity achieved by explicit instruction to the younger generation entering the priesthood. The druids' second function in Gaul was the practical application of their learning in law and to the administration of justice, though how this power operated side-by-side with that of the tribal chief or the *vergobretos* is nowhere explained. Finally, the druids supervised sacrifices and religious ceremonies in general, in which they and other functionaries (for instance *vates* or *manteis*) participated. Any divinatory powers they were believed to exercise would fall quite appropriately within their general priestly duties.

Stuart Piggott
The Druids, 1975

The Privilege of Knowledge

Once again it is Caesar who provides us with the most complete information on the status and role of the druids in Gaulish society in his day. The druids were the exclusive intellectual elite, and were recruited among the ranks of the nobility. They enjoyed special privileges, such as exemption from tributes and were not obliged to bear arms.... Their education was very lengthy, and involved twenty years of memorizing sacred texts which religious taboo banned from being put in writing. The druids were acquainted with writing, however.... In their religious role, the druids insured the conduct of religious practices, presided over sacrificial rites and received and interpreted omens. The only ones "to know the nature of the gods," they acted as intermediaries between the world of humankind and the domain of the supernatural. Guardians of the fundamental gnosis [knowledge of spiritual matters], they perpetuated a conception of mankind and the universe contained in an esoteric doctrine which, for obvious reasons, remains a mystery....

Deeply religious, the Celts believed in doing anything possible to insure the smooth running of the universe. Consequently, they did not hesitate to make human sacrifices when the situation made it necessary. They believed that if they failed to carry out the appropriate sacrifice in the allotted time, the worst would befall them.

Venceslas Kruta
"Celtic Religion"
The Celts, 1991

The druids take no part in war and do not pay tribute along with the others.... Attracted by such privileges, many [young Gauls] come for training of their own volition or are sent by their kinsmen and relatives. There they are said to learn large numbers of verses; some remain in training for twenty years. They do not believe it lawful to commit this lore to writing, and yet for most public and private purposes and accounts they do use Greek letters. It seems to me that there are two reasons for this practice: One is to prevent their knowledge spreading among common people, while the other is to prevent their students losing their memories by relying on writing.

Julius Caesar
Commentaries on the Gallic War
Book VI, 51 BC

Judges of the People

The druids did not form a hereditary caste but a clergy that was recruited from the most able people and had a high priest, councils, and the terrible weapon of excommunication. Their leader had boundless authority. "On his death, the foremost in dignity succeeds him; or, if several have equal claims, then a vote is held among the druids and the position is sometimes contested by force of arms. At a certain time of year all the druids assemble in a consecrated spot on the fringe of Carnutes territory [near Chartres, in northern central France], which is regarded as the central point in Gaul. People who have disputes gather there from every direction, and they submit to the judgments and decisions of the druids." In some places druids were still the judges of the people. "If some crime has been committed or a murder taken place, if there is conflict over an inheritance or over boundaries, it is they who give a ruling. They hand out compensations and penalties. If some individual...refuses to accept their decision they ban him from sacrifices: This is the most exquisite penalty among them. People who incur this ban are relegated to the ranks of the impious and criminals; everyone shuns them, avoiding talking with them as though they feared contagion from the ill that had befallen them. They are refused all access to justice, and have no share in any honor."

Victor Duruy,
History of the Romans, Vol. III, 1881,
quoting Caesar, *Commentaries on the Gallic War,* Book VI, 51 BC

The decoration of peculiar ritual spoons that appeared in Ireland in the 1st century AD suggests the partition of the universe. The spoons probably had a function in Celtic divination. This engraving of 1868 (opposite) depicts an oath taken by Gallic leaders in the Carnutes forest.

Celtic Gold

Celtic artisans working in gold not only created jewelry but also produced vessels and display weapons—often in solid gold—using an enormous amount of raw material. Greeks and Romans often remarked on the Celts' almost excessive taste for gold and their habit of wearing shiny ornaments on all occasions. The number and wealth of the Celtic deposits in Europe certainly were remarkable.

The Proceeds of Conquest

Caesar often spoke of "Gallia aurifera," or gold-bearing Gaul. Unfortunately most of this gold disappeared into Roman melting pots, as ancient texts describe. In Lives of the Twelve Caesars *the 1st-century AD biographer Suetonius says, "In Gaul [Caesar] plundered temples and sanctuaries of the gods filled with offerings and sacked towns more often to obtain booty than to punish rebellion. The result was that he had great quantities of gold which he had sold in Italy and the provinces at a price of 3000 sesterces to the pound." It is also thought that when Caesar conquered Gaul the relative value of silver to gold fell since the influx of gold served to lower its value. But this accumulation of wealth did not meet with general approval, and there were even those in whom it aroused shame, including the poet Valerius Catullus (84?–54 BC).*

Who but a wanton, gluttonous gambler could bear to watch Mamurra having the riches that Gaul and furthest Britain once possessed?...as he proudly struts like a fat white pigeon through people's bedrooms....

Valerius Catullus
Carmina, Poem 29, c. 60 BC

Deposits and Hoards

Diodorus Siculus explains how the Celts collected their gold.

In Gaul there is plenty of native gold that the inhabitants collect without difficulty or mining. As the rivers rush through their winding bends and dash against the foot of mountains they detach lumps of rock and become full of gold dust. People who do this work collect and break up the dust-bearing rocks, remove the earthy part by repeated washing, and melt the rest in furnaces. In this way they gather gold that is used for ornaments not only for women but for men as well, for they wear bracelets on their wrists and arms and also massive solid-gold collars around their necks, fine finger-rings, and even gold breastplates. The inland Celts make an unusual and surprising use of their temples. In sanctuaries and sacred enclosures in this area a lot of gold is openly displayed as offerings to the gods, and although the Celts have an excessive love of money, none of the natives dares touch it because of religious fear.

Diodorus Siculus
Historical Library, Book V, c. 50 BC

Gold torque and bracelets from the grave of the Waldalgesheim princess (below) and gold earrings from the Late Iron Age (opposite).

Strabo was impressed by the abundance of precious metals and the ease with which they were exploited.

[Lakes and sacred ponds offered especially safe repositories where gold and silver ingots were thrown as offerings to the gods]: When the Romans took control of the area they sold the lakes for revenues at public auction, and many of the people who purchased them found that they contained large ingots of beaten silver in the shape of millstones. And at Tolosa too there was a sacred temple, greatly revered by the surrounding populations, and because of that its wealth built up with many accumulated offerings, while nobody dared to lay a hand upon them.

Strabo
Geography, Book IV, c. AD 17

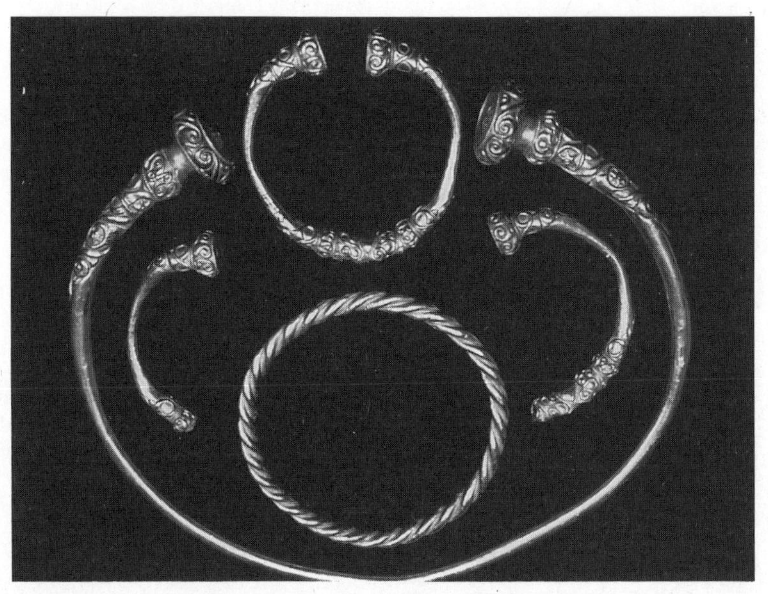

Celtic Art

The art of the Celts is their most enduring legacy. With its feeling for abstract pattern, use of spiral forms, and delicate undulating lines, it stands in marked contrast to the classical art of Greece and Rome. The Celtic style is still very much alive in decorative and applied art today.

Ways of Seeing

In dealing with Celtic art, it is necessary to abandon post-Renaissance definitions, which are as meaningless in understanding the Celts as they are for most other prehistoric or ethnographic material. Distinctions developed in our own society between "high art," popular art and craft are alien to most other peoples at most other times. In particular, the view that "real" art, as distinct from craft, must exist primarily in the realm of ideas, and have no demonstrable practical use, is a very modern concept. Much Celtic art is found on everyday objects—pottery, weapons and horse harnesses. Of surviving wooden carvings, many have the eminently practical purpose of asking a deity for help or healing. Stone carving is rare, and apparently also usually connected with religion, certainly with a system of ideas and beliefs, but one of which we have little real understanding.

The idea of an avant-garde group, regularly and consciously challenging the techniques or subject-matter of "established" art, is really a 19th-century invention not applicable to most traditional societies, where continuity is valued and preserved.... It is difficult even today to make generally accepted aesthetic judgments about objects from different cultures.... It may well be possible to assess technical skill or technical incompetence, but it is also possible that the Celts were sometimes more concerned with the symbolism of a motif on a scabbard or brooch than with the degree of skill with which it was carried out, the message being more important than the medium. Here we have another problem, for we cannot tell the precise meaning to a Celt of even some of the commonest motifs such as the three-armed triskel or whirligig or, amongst more obvious animal representations, the boar.... While not knowing the belief systems of Celtic society, we can still recognize repeated symbols, but we cannot fully understand them, or respond to them in the same way as did the Celts.

Ruth and Vincent Megaw,
Celtic Art: From Its Beginnings to the Book of Kells, 1989

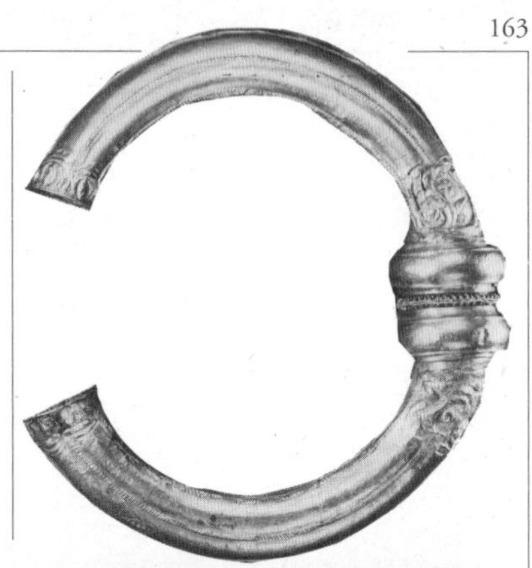

A gold tubular torque from northeastern France (top) and a 3rd-century BC torque from southern France (above). Detail of a handle on a 1st-century BC bronze-trimmed wooden bucket found in a cremation burial at Aylesford, Kent (opposite).

Celtic Art

Among the great works of art of the ancient world, many stand out as being uniquely Celtic. This art was developed in a temperate climate that fostered a sense of the mysterious allure of the forest and its powerful animals. It also favoured a fertile agricultural and stock-raising economy and provided a bountiful supply of water, and ample quantities of iron and stone. In their representations the Celts showed a clear preference for tribal goddesses, powerful beasts, imaginary monsters, strangely stylized animals and twisting, intertwined plants, while the male figure was all but ignored.... Plants had an almost religious importance in everyday life, and each year the druids gathered mistletoe, a solemn event that the Gauls took very seriously. Thus, the main features of Celtic art were closely tied to the most ancient forms of Celtic paganism, and were repeated with increasing frequency in the course of the half-millennium before Christ.

Paul-Marie Duval
"Celtic Art"
The Celts, 1991

Traditions of Celtic Art

In essence, there are three rather than two "traditions" of Celtic art. The first, continental La Tène art, started in the 5th century BC and continued until around the time of Caesar's conquest of Gaul in the 1st century BC. This art drew on native, classical and oriental sources (the last possibly derived second-hand from the Mediterranean) to produce a diversity of distinct but related styles. Although there is a certain amount of sculpture in stone and wood, most of the La Tène continental art that has come down to us was fashioned in metal, using a variety of techniques. Commonest is casting, but this can be combined with engraving, punching, tracing and scorping (grooving the metal with an implement known as a "scorper"). Compasses were on occasion used in laying out designs. Bronze was the commonest metal employed, but gold, silver and even iron was on occasion ornamented. Coral or glass were sometimes used to enhance the natural surface of the metal. Ground was sometimes cut away to form openwork.

The second tradition is in some measure dependent on and derivative of the first, and comprises the La Tène art produced in Britain and Ireland from the 5th or 4th century BC until the Roman conquest by Claudius in AD 43 (or somewhat later in areas outside Roman control). Many of the elements of this "Insular" La Tène art are shared in common with the Continent, but the creations are mostly distinctive and represent regional styles of the La Tène tradition. The materials and substances employed are much the same, but British craftsmen showed a particular liking for basket patterns for infilling ground, and for enamelwork.

The third tradition of Celtic art is

This sheet-bronze stylized horse's head was found in a Stanwick (Yorkshire) hoard with other chariot and horse trappings.

that which flourished in Ireland and to a lesser extent Britain between the 5th and 12th centuries AD. This art borrows heavily from Roman motifs, and it is a debated point as to what extent it owes a debt to La Tène art at all. From modest beginnings in later Roman Britain it was transmitted to Ireland in the 5th century and from the 6th flourished on Irish soil. Except by the Picts and Scots of northern Scotland, little Celtic art of note seems to have been produced in Britain after the 7th century. Of this "Dark Age" Celtic art, most that has survived is in metal and stone, though a few rare pieces of woodwork show that this too was ornamented. A new medium however came to the fore—the illuminated manuscript. The range of ornamental techniques of the Iron Age artist was greatly extended by his post-Roman counterpart: Gold filigree and granular work and the technique of cloisonné inlaying were developed in response to similar techniques employed by contemporary Germanic artists, while die-stamped foils and new materials such as niello (a black silver sulphide paste) were added to the repertoire.

The Norman penetration of Celtic Britain and Ireland seems to have led to the disappearance of Celtic art in the 13th century. Although elements of a Celtic tradition can be detected from time to time thereafter, it was not until the conscious revival of Celtic art in the 19th century that it became popular again. The factors behind its revival, particularly in Ireland, were originally partly at least political, but it rapidly appealed as an ornamental form to those who had little or no concern for issues of nationalism, and to judge by the proliferation of objects decorated in Celtic style, it has not yet outlived its vogue.

Lloyd and Jennifer Laing
Art of the Celts, 1992

This 1st-century BC gold torque comes from Snettisham, Norfolk, an area known as the territory of the Iceni, whose queen was Boudicea.

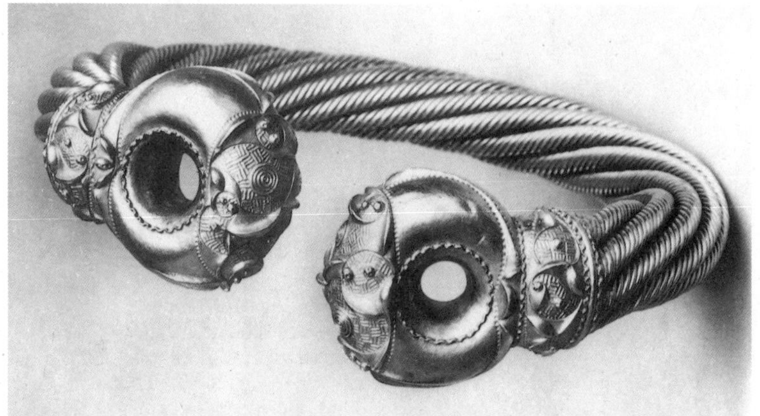

The First British Heroine

Our only sources for the story of the Celts' resistance to Rome are Roman historians—including Cornelius Tacitus (c. 56–c. 120)—but even they are obliged to concede the heroism of leaders such as Vercingetorix in Gaul and Caractacus in Britain. No figure seizes the imagination so much, however, as the warrior queen Boudicea, who took over the rule of the Iceni, a tribe in Norfolk, and led a rebellion in AD *61 that cost Rome its chief town in the southeast and thousands of her subjects' lives.*

The Rebellion Against the Romans

Suetonius [the Roman general in command of Britain]…received tidings of the sudden revolt of the province. Prasutagus, king of the Iceni, famed for his long prosperity, had made the emperor his heir along with his two daughters, under the impression that this token of submission would put his kingdom and his house out of the reach of wrong. But the reverse was the result, so much so that his kingdom was plundered by centurions, his house by slaves, as if they were the spoils of war. First, Boudicea [Prasutagus's wife] was scourged and his daughters outraged. All the chief men of the Iceni…were stript of their ancestral possessions, and the king's relatives were made slaves. Roused by these insults and the dread of worse, reduced as they now were into the condition of a province, they flew to arms.…

Suetonius had the fourteenth legion with the veterans of the twentieth, and auxiliaries from the neighbourhood, to the number of about ten thousand armed men, when he prepared to fight a battle.… On the other side, the army of the Britons…was…so fierce in spirit that they actually brought with them, to witness the victory, their wives riding in wagons, which they had placed on the extreme border of the plain.

Boudicea, with her daughters before her in a chariot, went up to tribe after tribe, protesting that it was indeed usual for Britons to fight under the leadership of women. "But now," she said, "it is not as a woman descended from noble ancestry, but as one of the people that I am avenging lost freedom, my scourged body, the outraged chastity of my daughters. Roman lust has gone

Sculpture of Boudicea in London (above) and a coin used by the Iceni tribe (opposite).

so far that not our very persons, nor even age or virginity, are left unpolluted. But heaven is on the side of a righteous vengeance; a legion which dared to fight has perished; the rest are hiding themselves in their camp, or are thinking anxiously of flight. They will not sustain even the din and the shout of so many thousands, much less our charge and our blows. If you weigh well the strength of the armies, and the causes of the war, you will see that in this battle you must conquer or die. This is a woman's resolve; as for men, they may live and be slaves."…

Suetonius gave the signal of battle. At first, the legion kept its position…when they had exhausted their missiles, which they discharged with unerring aim on the closely approaching foe, they rushed out in a wedge-like column. Similar was the onset of the auxiliaries, while the cavalry with extended lances broke through all who offered a strong resistance. The rest turned their back in flight, and flight proved difficult, because the surrounding wagons had blocked retreat. Our soldiers spared not to slay even the women, while the very beasts of burden, transfixed by the missiles, swelled the piles of bodies. Great glory …was won on that day. Some…say that there fell little less than eighty thousand of the Britons, with a loss to our soldiers of about four hundred, and only as many wounded. Boudicea put an end to her life by poison.

The Annals of Tacitus, Book XIV
translated by Alfred J. Church and
William J. Brodribb, 1876

Further Reading

Allen, Derek F., and Daphne Nash, *The Coins of the Ancient Celts,* Columbia University Press, New York, 1980

The Book of Kells, facsimile edition, Abrams, New York, 1991

de Breffny, Brian, *The Land of Ireland,* Abrams, New York, 1979

Brunaux, Jean-Louis, *The Celtic Gauls: Gods, Rites and Sanctuaries,* Numismatic Fine Arts, Los Angeles, 1988

Chadwick, Nora, *The Celts,* Penguin, New York, 1971

Cunliffe, Barry W., *The Celtic World,* Crown, New York, 1986

———, *Iron Age Communities in Britain,* Routledge Chapman and Hall, New York, 1991

Duval, Paul-Marie, and Christopher F. C. Hawkes, eds., *Celtic Art in Ancient Europe: Five Protohistoric Centuries,* Academic Press, San Diego, 1976

Green, Miranda J., *Dictionary of Celtic Myth and Legend,* Thames and Hudson, New York, 1992

———, *The Gods of the Celts,* Barnes and Noble Imports, Savage, Maryland, 1986

———, *Symbol and Image in Celtic Religious Art,* Routledge Chapman and Hall, New York, 1992

Groenewegen-Frankfort, H. A., and Bernard Ashmole, *Art of the Ancient World,* Abrams, New York, 1971

James, Simon, *The World of the Celts,* Thames and Hudson, New York, 1993

Kruta, Venceslas, Otto Hermann Frey, Miklós Szabó, and Barry Raftery, eds., *The Celts,* Rizzoli, New York, 1991

Laing, Lloyd, and Jennifer Laing, *Art of the Celts,* Thames and Hudson, New York, 1992

MacCana, Proinsias, *Celtic Mythology,* Peter Bedrick Books, New York, 1991

Megaw, Ruth, and Vincent Megaw, *Celtic Art: From Its Beginnings to the Book of Kells,* Thames and Hudson, New York, 1989

Piggott, Stuart, *The Druids,* Thames and Hudson, New York, 1975

Powell, T. G. E., *The Celts,* Thames and Hudson, New York, 1983

Raftery, Barry, *Celtic Art,* Abbeville, New York, 1991

Rees, Alwyn, and Brinley Rees, *Celtic Heritage: Ancient Traditions in Ireland and Wales,* Thames and Hudson, New York, 1989

Ryan, Kathleen J., and Bernard Share, eds., *Irish Traditions,* Abrams, New York, 1990

Sandars, Nancy K., *Prehistoric Art in Europe,* Yale University Press, New Haven, Connecticut, 1992

Sharkey, John, *Celtic Mysteries: The Ancient Religion,* Thames and Hudson, New York, 1975

Sheehy, Jeanne, *The Rediscovery of Ireland's Past: The Celtic Revival, 1830–1930,* Thames and Hudson, New York, 1980

Stead, I. M., *Early Celtic Art,* Harvard University Press, Cambridge, Massachusetts, 1985

Youngs, Susan, ed., *The Work of Angels: Masterpieces of Celtic Metalwork, 6th to 9th Centuries AD,* University of Texas Press, Austin, 1989

List of Illustrations

Abbreviations: ***a***=above; ***b***=below; ***c***=center; ***l***=left; ***r***=right; BM=British Museum, London; BN=Bibliothèque Nationale, Paris; MAN=Musée des Antiquités Nationales, St.-Germain-en-Laye, France; NM=Naturhistorisches Museum, Vienna; WL=Württembergisches Landesmuseum, Stuttgart

Front cover Detail from the Gundestrup cauldron (Denmark). 1st century AD. National Museum of Copenhagen

Spine Sandstone statue of the god Janus from Holzgerlingen (Germany). c. 6th or 5th century BC. Landesdenkmalamt, Baden-Württemberg, Germany

Back cover Helmet found in the Thames River (England). 1st century AD. BM

1 Bronze mask of a male deity from Montserié (Hautes-Pyrénées, France). 1st century BC. Musée Massey, Tarbes, France

2–3 Mask ornament on a funerary casket from the Kleinklein tumulus (Austria). 7th century BC. Landesmuseum Joanneum, Graz, Austria

4 Bronze figure (42 cm high) from Bouray (Essonne, France). c. 1st century AD. MAN

5 Stone man's head (23.5 cm high), from Bohemia. 2nd–1st century BC. Národní Muzeum, Prague

6–7 Sculpture called the two-headed Hermes of Roquepertuse (Bouches-du-Rhône, France). 3rd–2nd centuries BC. Musée de la Vieille Charité, Marseilles, France
8–9 Stylized heads from a pillar found at Entremont. 2nd century BC. Musée d'Aix-en-Provence, France
11 Bronze figurines from the Balzers sanctuary (Liechtenstein). 3rd–1st centuries BC. Landesmuseum, Vaduz, Liechtenstein
12 Charles Royer. *Grave at La Motte-St.-Valentin* (Haute-Marne, France). Oil on canvas, 1884. Musée d'Orsay, Paris
13 Bronze figurine from the Hallstatt cemetery (Austria). NM
14l Sandstone grave marker with bas-reliefs from Pfalzfeld (Germany). 450–350 BC. Rheinisches Landesmuseum, Bonn
14r Cauldron from Podmokly (former Czechoslovakia). Engraving, 1771
15a Lake at the Hallstatt site. Photograph
15b Lake of Neuchâtel, site of La Tène (Switzerland). Photograph
16a Early Iron Age barrow at Kilchberg, Tübingen (Baden-Württemberg, Germany). Photograph
16l Funerary urn from Sublaines (Indre-et-Loire, France). MAN
16–7 Breastplate from Marmesse (Haute-Marne, France). 9th–8th centuries BC. MAN
17r Bronze pectoral from Les Moidons (Jura, France). MAN
18l Ax head from Hallstatt. 7th century BC. Watercolor. MAN library
18r Bronze ax head from Hallstatt. 7th century BC. NM
18–9 Drawing of a 5th-century BC sword scabbard from Hallstatt
19a Detail of a sword scabbard from Hallstatt. 5th century BC. NM
20a Bronze cordon cist from Montceau-Laurent barrow at Magny-Lambert (Côte-d'Or, France). 8th century BC. MAN
20b Bronze fibulae from Hallstatt, seen from above and below. c. 7th century BC. NM
21 Iron swords with long blades and other weapons from Hallstatt. 7th century BC. Watercolor. MAN library
22 Miner's shoe from Dürrnberg, near Hallein (Salzburg, Austria). Museum Carolino Augusteum, Salzburg
23 Excavations directed by the grand duchess of Mecklenburg at Hallstatt in 1907. Photograph
24–5 Isidor Engel. The excavations at the Hallstatt site. Watercolor drawings in Johann Georg Ramsauer, "Protokoll Ramsauer," 1846. NM
26–7a and c Views of the Hallstatt mine. MAN library
26bl Torch for lighting the mine galleries at Hallstatt. NM
26br Pick and stone from the Dürrnberg salt mine, Hallein. Museum Carolino Augusteum, Salzburg
27b Knapsack for carrying salt from the Hallstatt mine. NM
28 Detail from the bronze couch in the prince's tomb at Hochdorf (Germany). 6th century BC. WL
29 The Hirschlanden warrior, an anthropomorphic grave marker from a barrow at Baden-Württemberg (Germany). 6th century BC. WL
30 The citadel of Hohenasperg (Baden-Württemberg, Germany). Photograph
30–1 François Place. Map of principal Celtic sites in the 6th century BC.
31b Terra-cotta amphora from Mercey (Haute-Saône, France). MAN
32 Jar from Grächwill (Bern, Switzerland). c. 570 BC. Historisches Museum, Bern
33al Plan of the Heuneburg citadel (Baden-Württemberg Germany). Drawing by Wolfgang Kimmig
33ar Sun-dried brick wall at the Heuneburg. Photograph
33c Drawing of a satyr's head on a wine flagon handle from the Heuneburg
34a Sketch of the funeral chamber of the Hohmichele barrow (Germany)
34–5 Reconstruction of a funerary wagon. Prähistorische Staatssammlung, Munich
35a Josef Mosbrugger. *Excavation of the Kaltbrunn Barrow.* Oil on canvas, 1864. Rosgartenmuseum, Constance, Germany
35cr Plan of an Iron Age barrow
36l Embossed gold-leaf decoration from the Hochdorf prince's shoes. 6th century BC. WL
36b The Hochdorf prince's skull. WL
36–7 Bronze couch from the Hochdorf prince's tomb. 6th century BC. WL
37r Detail of a bronze foot (35 cm high) with coral decoration from the Hochdorf couch. 6th century BC. WL
38a Iron and gold drinking horn from the Hochdorf tomb. 6th century BC. WL
38b Drawing of an imported cauldron with griffins and tripod
39a Drawing of the Hochdorf tomb and its furnishings
39b Top of a bronze cauldron with three lions and three handles from the Hochdorf tomb. 6th century BC. WL
40a Flask with four feet from Dürrnberg. 5th century BC. Keltenmuseum, Hallein, Austria
40c Bronze wine flagon from Ca' Morta (Como, Italy). Museo Civico Archeologico Giovio, Como, Italy
40bl Gold bracelets and pin heads from a woman's tomb at Ditzingen-Schöckingen (Baden-Württemberg, Germany). 6th century BC. WL
40br Bead and chain from the Ins barrow (Bern, Switzerland). Historisches Museum, Bern
41a Gold bead and pendant from the Jegenstorf barrow (Switzerland). Historisches Museum, Bern
41b Gold torque from the Uttendorf barrow (Austria). 6th century BC. Oberösterreichisches Landesmuseum, Linz, Austria
42a Reconstruction of the head of the Vix princess. Musée Archéologique, Châtillon-sur-Seine, France

100–1b Knives and sheepshears. 3rd–2nd century BC. Musée Cantonal d'Archéologie, Neuchâtel, Switzerland
101a Reconstruction of a Celtic village near Quin, Ireland
101cr Drawing of a potter's kiln
102 Sculpted pillar (detail) from the Entremont sanctuary (Bouches-du-Rhône, France). 2nd century BC. Musée Granet, Aix-en-Provence, France
103 Statue of a warrior god from St.-Maur-en-Chaussée (Oise, France). 1st century BC. Musée Départemental de l'Oise, Beauvais
104l Wooden statue of stag from a cult pit at Fellbach-Schmiden (Germany). 2nd century BC. Landesdenkmalamt, Baden-Württemberg, Germany
104r and 105r Drawings of funerary shafts at Bernard-en-Vendée
104–5b Iron swords from the sanctuary of Gournay-sur-Aronde (Oise, France). 3rd century BC. Musée Vivenal, Compiègne, France
106 Horse skeleton from Côte-d'Or (France). Photograph
106–7 Aerial view of the sanctuary of Ribemont-sur-Ancre (Somme, France). Photograph
107 Ossuary column at Ribemont-sur-Ancre. Site photograph
108al Stone sculpture of a severed head gripped by a warrior's hand from Entremont. 2nd century BC. Musée Granet, Aix-en-Provence, France
108r Statue of a squatting warrior from the Entremont sanctuary. 2nd century BC. Musée Granet, Aix-en-Provence, France
109a Pillar decorated with stylized heads from Entremont. Musée Granet, Aix-en-Provence, France
109b Severed head set in a pillar niche from Roquepertuse (Bouches-du-Rhône, France). 3rd century BC. Musée de la Vieille Charité, Marseilles, France
110b Gold boat from the Broighter treasure (Northern Ireland). 1st century BC. National Museum of Ireland, Dublin
110r and 111l Wooden statues representing pilgrims, votive offerings from the source of the Seine (Côte-d'Or, France). 1st century BC. Musée Archéologique, Dijon, France
111r Bronze dancing girl from Neuvy-en-Sullias (Loiret, France). 1st century BC. Musée d'Orléans
112 Cult branch in wood and bronze with gold leaf from the oppidum of Manching (Bavaria, Germany). 3rd or 2nd century BC. Prähistorische Staatssammlung, Munich
112–3 Gold coins from Bavaria (Germany). Prähistorische Staatssammlung, Munich
113 God found at Euffigneix (Haute-Marne, France). Late 1st century BC. MAN
114l Carved stone from the Nautes Parisiacae monument (detail representing the god Esus). Engraving. BN
114–5 Stone sculpture of two heads joined at the back from the Roquepertuse sanctuary. 3rd century BC. Musée Borély, Marseilles, France
115b Bronze statuette of the goddess Artio with her bear from Muri (Switzerland). Historisches Museum, Bern
116–7 Cauldron (whole object and details) from Gundestrup. 1st century BC. National Museum of Copenhagen
118al and cr Carved stone from the Nautes Parisiacae monument (details representing the gods Tarvos Trigaranus and Cernunnos). Engraving. BN
118–9a Druids collecting mistletoe. 19th-century engraving
120 Page from the *Book of Kells.* St. Matthew's gospel, with the Greek initials of the name of Christ. c. 800 AD. Trinity College, Dublin
121 Stone statuette of a deity from Paule, near St.-Brieuc (Côtes-d'Armor, France). c. 70 BC. Nouveau Musée, St-Brieuc, France
122 The Dorty cross at Kilfenora (Ireland). 12th century AD
123a Page from the *Book of Durrow* showing the figure of St. Matthew. c. 675 AD. Trinity College, Dublin
123b The gilded silver Tara brooch (detail) from Bettystown (Country Meath, Ireland). 8th century AD. National Museum of Ireland, Dublin
124a Manuscript of laws, an extract concerning the rights of women. Large-character text dates from the 8th century. Smaller writing shows comments added in the 12th century. Trinity College, Dublin
124–5 Aerial view of a horse cut into the chalk at Uffington (Oxfordshire). Photograph
125r Charles-Auguste Herbé. *Bard Singing and Gauls from Narbonne Ready for Battle.* Lithograph, 19th century
126a Druids burning their victims in a wicker colossus. A still from Robin Hardy's film *The Wicker Man,* 1973
126b Human sacrifice among the Gauls. Engraving in Aylett Sammes, *Britannia Antiqua Illustrata,* 1676
127 Anne-Louis Girodet. *Ossian Receives the Souls of Heroes Who Died for Their Country.* Oil on canvas, 19th century. Salon Doré de la Malmaison, Paris
128 Detail of a wine flagon handle from the tomb of the Waldalgesheim princess. 4th century BC. Rheinisches Landes-museum, Bonn
129 Bronze cow's-head bucket fitting from Felmersham-on-Ouse (Bedfordshire). c. 1st century AD. Bedford Museum, Bedford
130 The geographer Strabo. Engraving, 17th century
132 Map compiled in 1933 by A. Berthelot from Strabo's descriptions
134 Stone statue that stood on a barrow. 6th century BC
135 Man's head (23.5 cm high) from Bohemia. 2nd–1st century BC. Národní Muzeum, Prague, Czech Republic
137 Stone statue of a warrior from the barrow at Hirschlanden (Baden-Württemberg, Germany). 6th century BC. WL
138 A Gallic family. Engraving, 19th century
140–1 A Gallic banquet. Engraving, 19th century
143 Iron bull's-head firedog and frame from a

grave at Welwyn (Hertfordshire). c. 50–10 BC. BM
144 Ogham stone at Castlekeeran (Ireland)
145 Drawing showing how ogham script characters can be identified on stones
146 Lepontic alphabet
146–7 Palm of a hand in bronze with Iberian inscription from Contrebia (Spain). 1st century BC. BN, Cabinet des Médailles
147a Stone plaque with Gallo-Greek inscriptions. 2nd or 1st century BC. Musée Calvet, Avignon, France
148 Helmet from Casino Pallavicino. Museo Archeologico Nazionale, Parma, Italy
149 John White. Celtic warrior. Watercolor, 1590
150 Early Gallic gold coin depicting chariot scene. BN, Cabinet des Médailles
151 Reconstruction of a British war chariot. National Museum of Wales, Cardiff
152 E. Frémiet. Gallic horseman. Bronze statue. MAN
153 Decorated sword with human head, iron blade, and bronze sheath found at Tesson (Charente-Maritime, France). lst century BC. MAN
154 The druids' grove. A set for Vincenzo Bellini's opera *Norma,* 1831. Engraving. Bibliothèque de l'Opéra, Paris
156 Druids on the island of Sein, off the northwest coast of France. Engraving, 19th century
157 Druids gathering sacred mistletoe. Engraving, 19th century
158 G. Durand. Gallic leaders taking an oath in the forest of the Carnutes, France. Engraving, 1868
159 Bronze ritual spoons from Ireland. 1st century AD. National Museum of Ireland, Dublin
160 Gold earrings from the Late Iron Age. MAN
161 Gold torque and bracelets from the princess's grave at Waldalgesheim. Late 4th century BC. Rheinisches Landesmuseum, Bonn
162 Head from the handle of the bronze-trimmed wooden bucket from Aylesford (Kent). lst century BC. BM
163a Gold tubular torque from Mailly-le-Camp (Aube, France). Late 2nd–early 1st century BC. MAN
163b Torque from Fenouillet (Haute-Garonne, France). 3rd century BC. Musée St.-Raymond, Toulouse, France
164 Sheet-bronze horse-head mount from Stanwick (Yorkshire). 1st century AD. BM
165 The Snettisham torque from Norfolk. 1st century BC. BM
166 Coin of the Iceni tribe. BM
167 Thomas Thornycroft. Sculpture of Boudicea on the Thames Embankment, London, 1902. The British Tourist Authority, London

Index

Page numbers in italic refer to captions and/or illustrations

Acknowledgments

The author would like to thank Michel Comode, Dr. Jörg Biel, and the management of the Württembergisches Museum in Stuttgart, Germany

Photograph Credits

R. Agache 106–7. All rights reserved 14r, 30, 30–1, 33al, 33ar, 33cl, 34a, 35cr, 36b, 38b, 39a, 49a, 64a, 77r, 84, 85, 87b, 88a, 114l, 118al, 118cr, 122, 124a, 126a, 132, 135, 137, 145, 146, 149. Archiv für Kunst und Geschichte, Berlin 13, 18–9, 27b, 46b, 48–9, 48, 49b, 92b, back cover. Artephot/Faillet, Paris 111r. Bedford Museum, Bedford 129. Bibliothèque Nationale, Paris 87a, 154. Suzanne Bosman, London 95bl. Bridgeman Art Library, London 123a, 123b. British Museum, London 94, 95a, 143, 162, 164, 165, 166. British Tourist Authority 167. Centre Archéologique de Compiègne/Patrice Mériel 106. Centre de Recherche Archéologique, Université d'Amiens/J.-L. Cadoux 107. J.-L. Charmet, Paris 80–1, 126b. Michel Comode 66. Dagli Orti, Paris 4, 40c, 42bl, 42br, 43a, 43c, 50, 101a, 101cr. Jean Dieuzaide 1, 74l, 163b. Dorka 156, 157. Editions Fabbri-Bompiani, Milan 5, 26br, 56a, 56b, 58a, 59a, 60a, 60bl, 63, 65b, 68–9, 70a, 72a, 74r, 95br, 98–9a, 100–1b, 103, 104–5b, 109a, 147a. Mary Evans Picture Library/Explorer, Paris 93. Flinders University of South Australia, Adelaide 58bl and 58br. Giraudon, Paris 73, 88b, 89b, 120. Claus Hansmann 34–5, 47ar, 112. Historisches Museum, Basel 97b. Historisches Museum, Bern 32, 98l, 115b. Historisches Museum der Pfalz, Speyer 55, 60–1a. Ikoni/V. Grousson, Paris 125r. Camille Jullian/CNRS, Aix-en-Provence 81b, 109b, 114–5. Gilbert Kaenel-P. Curdy 83bl, 83br. Karbine/Tapabor, Paris 118–9a. Keltenmuseum, Hallein 51, 53b. Bernard Lambot 100l. Landesdenkmalamt, Baden-Württemberg 16a, 28, 38a, 104l, spine. Landesinstitut für Pädagogik und Medien, Dudweiler, Germany 60–1b. E. Lessing/Magnum 2–3, 15a, 15b, 18r, 19a, 20a, 20b, 22, 24–5, 26bl, 36–7, 37r, 40a, 40bl, 40br, 41a, 41b, 45a, 45b, 46a, 52–3, 54–5, 62, 69b, 110r, 111l, 128. Liechtensteinisches Landesmuseum, Vaduz 11. Magyar Nemzeti Múzeum, Budapest 72a. MAN, St.-Germain-en-Laye 16l, 17r, 18l, 21, 23, 26–7a, 26–7c, 44, 52a, 53a, 56a, 56b, 57b, 61b, 71a, 76a, 84–5. J.-P. Mohen 42a. Musée Bargoin, Clermont-Ferrand 86l. Musée Calvet, Avignon 146–7. Musée des Beaux-Arts/Gilbert Mangin, Nancy 65a. Musée des Beaux-Arts/J+M, La Rochelle 67. Musée des Beaux-Arts/P. Cartier, Carcassonne 78. Musée des Beaux-Arts/P. Kempf, Mulhouse 82–3, 89a. Musée des Jacobins/Alain le Nouail, Morlaix 77l. Museo Archeologico Nazionale, Parma 148. Museu Nacional de Arqueologia e Etnologia, Lisbon 76b. Muzeul National de Istorie, Bucharest 68. National Museum of Ireland, Dublin 110b, 159. National Museum of Wales, Cardiff 151. Nouveau Musée, St-Brieuc 121. Patrimoine 2001/E. Brissaud, Paris 6–7, 8, 9, 70b, 80al, 82b, 90–1, 96–7, 98–9b, 102, 108al, 108r, 116–7, 134, 137, 161, front cover. Prähistorischen Staatssammlung, Munich 59b. Rapho/Geister 124–5. Rheinisches Landesmuseum, Bonn 61c. RMN, Paris 12, 16–7, 31b, 57a, 72b, 79, 86r, 96, 97c, 113, 127, 152, 153. Roger-Viollet, Paris 130, 138, 140–1, 144, 158. Römisch-Germanische Kommission des Deutsches Archäologischen Institut, Frankfurt 112–3. Rosgartenmuseum, Constance 35a. Scala 14l, 75. Staatliche Museum Antikensammlung Preussischer Kulturbesitz, Berlin 54a, 54b, 64b. Steiermärkisches Landesmuseum Joanneum, Graz 46–7. Tallandier, Paris 104r, 105r, 163a. University of Cambridge 92a. University of Ljubljana 70–1. Württembergisches Landesmuseum, Stuttgart 29, 36l, 39b, 60al

Text Credits

Grateful acknowledgment is made for permission to use material from Stuart Piggott, *The Druids,* © 1968 and 1975 Stuart Piggott (pp. 139–40 and 157–8)

Christiane Eluère is chief curator of the French national museums. At the Musée des Antiquités Nationales, in St.-Germain-en-Laye, she shares responsibility for the protohistoric collections. In 1987 Eluère helped organize the exhibition "Treasures of the Celtic Princes." Her publications include *Les Ors Préhistoriques* (1982), *L'Or des Celtes* (1987), and *Secrets de l'Or Antique* (1990).

Translated from the French by Daphne Briggs

Project Manager: Sharon AvRutick
Typographic Designer: Elissa Ichiyasu
Assistant Editor: Jennifer Stockman
Design Assistant: Penelope Hardy

Library of Congress Catalog Card Number: 93–70486

ISBN 0–8109–2852–3

Published in 1993 by Harry N. Abrams, Incorporated, New York

Printed and bound in Italy by Editoriale Lloyd, Trieste